From Hell to Glory

One Mother's Fight to Free Herself and Her Son from the Mafia's Lifestyle

Rosanne Cutrone

Clovercroft Publishing

*This book is dedicated to my Savior Jesus Christ
for never giving up on me.*

*To David and Barbara and their family for seeing who I was
in the kingdom, even though I could not.*

*To my son for being the biggest joy and gift from God:
being his mother, I have learned how to love, and how to be kind,
compassionate, and have patience in all circumstances.*

*To my parents for their life of hard knocks that taught me
how to survive my life to come.*

"But as many as received him, to them gave he power to become the sons of God, even to them that believe on his name" (John 1:12, KJV).

This is the testimony of the miracles that have occurred in my life since I have come to trust, honor, and obey my Lord and Savior Jesus Christ.

May this testimony let the world know that all things are possible for those who take the Lord Jesus into their hearts and believe in Him. He is real, and we who love Him can feel Him in our spirit as He covers us in the warmth of his love and serenity during all the trials of our lives.

"The LORD, will go before thee; he will be with thee, he will not fail thee, neither forsake thee: fear not, neither be dismayed" (Deuteronomy 31:8, KJV).

Some names have not been given in this book; I do not want to offend or put anyone in a light that they do not wish to be in. All has been forgiven, and we have all moved on.

From Hell to Glory: One Mother's Fight to Free Herself and Her Son from the Mafia's Lifestyle

©2016 by Rosanne Cutrone

Independently published by the author through Clovercroft Publishing, Franklin, Tennessee

Published in association with Larry Carpenter of Christian Book Services, LLC of Franklin, Tennessee

Cover Design by Suzanne Lawing

Interior Layout Design by Adept Content Solutions

ISBN: 978-1-942587-43-9

Printed in the United States of America

Contents

Acknowledgments vii

Preface ix

One
The Beginning 1

Two
More Early Years in Brooklyn 11

Three
God and Life in a Connected Family 17

Four
Life in Kerhonkson, New York 25

Five
Moving to Canarsie, New York 31

Six
High School Days 35

Seven
Starting to Work 39

Eight
My World Takes a Drastic Turn 45

Nine
Beginning to Walk and Live Again **49**

Ten
Freedom and a Fresh Start **53**

Eleven
Giving Love and Marriage Another Chance **57**

Twelve
On the Run **73**

Thirteen
Facing the Charges in Camden County, New Jersey **89**

Fourteen
Death of My Parents **95**

Fifteen
Beating Cancer and Starting Over ... Again **101**

Sixteen
A New Opportunity, a Fresh Start **111**

Seventeen
My Journey with God and Hearing from Him **115**

Eighteen
Learning to Depend on Jesus **123**

Nineteen
A New Beginning **137**

Twenty
Reflections of My Journey with Jesus **145**

Acknowledgments

I would like to thank my Lord Jesus Christ, because without Him I would not be alive today. After all the years of healing and getting to know the Lord, I am finally healed in body, mind, and spirit. I believe in my full restoration from the illnesses I have battled since I was born. As of the writing of this book, all fourteen autoimmune illnesses are in remission.

Preface

As I walk with the Lord, I often hear people say, "There is no God," or "Miracles do not happen anymore." But once I tell you this story, you will not only know Jesus is alive, you will know that He can be with every one of us every day. When times of trouble plague us, it is a matter of us running to Him and reaching out for his help to receive his grace.

I am not a writer, nor am I any sort of "perfect Christian." A thought came into my spirit as I was writing: *I am not a perfect representation of Jesus Christ, but I am a perfect representation of the sinner Jesus Christ loved and died to save, heal, and give eternal life to in the kingdom of God. He does all this by his grace when our time comes to go home to Him.* I do know I am saved, spiritually healed, and cleansed of my sins. I have eternal salvation through the death and resurrection of God's only begotten Son, Jesus Christ, who had to wrap himself in flesh to come to earth to be brutally beaten, humiliated, and die so we could be saved. With all the evil from the world in us, there is no other way we can approach God except through the salvation of Jesus Christ.

God our Father loves us but will not force us to choose Him. He leaves it to us whether we will be with Him.

As I grow and learn what having a relationship with Jesus means, I have come to trust the Holy Spirit more than any other person on the face of the planet.

I have started to write this book so many times, and I have not felt right about the content. This book is not being written to become famous, rich, or to bash those who have hurt me. It is being written to give hope to others so they may see Jesus as I have, so that He can bring those who have had a similar life of violence, neglect, and abuse home to his kingdom. I'm not saying that once Jesus came into my life it became easier. What I am saying is that with Jesus on my side I have been able to turn over the impossible in my life to *his* possible—and beyond.

This is one woman's story of how I made it out of the hell I called my life and into the peace, freedom, and happiness I call my life today.

One

The Beginning

Premature at four pounds and six ounces, my life began with a fight, and that fight has continued to this day. On a hot summer's day in August 1960 I was born in Brooklyn, New York. My parents were both born in the U.S. not long after their parents arrived from Italy.

Both families had strong ties to connected families from the old country; most of them emigrated here together on the same vessel. Both sets of my grandparents arrived around the same time at Ellis Island in New York City. Both families, although not knowing each other, came to live in Manhattan along with thousands of other immigrants from around the world; they were simply looking for a better life for their families. America was the shining light for the Lord and represented freedom for every man, woman, and child.

My parents' families were large, with five boys and four girls on my father's side, and three boys and two girls on my mother's side. My grandparents ruled with the iron fists of anger, discipline, and violence, which was the normal, everyday way to fight to survive in the new lifestyle of this country.

My parents had me late in life. I was an unplanned child. My mother and father had previous families. I found out about this when I was snooping through their off-limits Chinese table that held their important papers; I was about 9 when I learned this truth. In the table I found out my mother had two previous marriages and three children between them; one of these children I knew as my stepbrother, and he came to live with us for a time in the late 1960s. Her other two children I did not know; I only saw a picture of them. I knew of one of my father's children and the story behind her birth. But the family would not let me meet her until my father and mother passed away in 1996 and 1998. At that point, no one could stop me from meeting her. It was a great reunion; we talked for hours and had much in common. However, my sister knew who I was, but was not allowed to tell me her identity.

It wasn't until I was in my fifties that I found out the truth about my father's first marriage and a sister I never met. My father's divorce from his first wife didn't take place until 1962, so he was married to another woman at the time of my conception and birth.

My parents met in a restaurant in 1959; this was where my mother worked. My father and his friends came in often for meals throughout the week, and as the story goes they met, became friends, and started to date. When my mother found out she was pregnant, my parents moved in together, though neither of them had the desire to get married. Still, my father took responsibility and my family was created. But deceptions would go on in the family until the 1980s.

When I was born it was undeniable that I was my father's; I looked just like my father, only I had thick black hair and he was bald. The pictures I have acquired since my mother and father passed away show me another side of them and their families. This is a side I rarely saw.

In Italian families that have mob ties, it's all about respect, honor, and secrets. A picture of my father holding me when I was brought home from the hospital looks like he is angry and I am infectious! My butt is in one hand and his fingers are around the back of my neck, holding my head up as he holds me away from his body. This picture told the story; if he had to have another kid, he wanted a boy, which I was not.

They were a striking couple, and in the beginning when they were out with their friends—who, by the way, were also in the "family"—it looked like all were having fun. Eventually, I began to warm up my father's heart and he began to love me. I don't think he had a choice since I looked exactly like him. It was like the phrase: I became "daddy's little girl." After a while he toted me around to all of his meetings and visits to friends homes. Growing up, the resemblance drove my mother crazy. She let me know after every fight they had that I was always the one to blame for them being together.

I lived in a physically, mentally, and verbally abusive home. My home was a hotbed of tempers, pride, and arrogance. My mother was always running away from my father, but he would always find us and bring us back home. Even though he showed me love, it was not like other families. It had terms, or conditions, and as long as my behavior conformed to the way they thought they should be raising a child, I was a "good Daddy's little girl" and "Mommy's darling." *When you grow up in a violent atmosphere, it becomes normal. It is not until you grow and become aware of how other families treat each other that you realize your family is different.*

My mother tried to dress me like a little doll with banana curls and crinoline dresses. The professional pictures I have of that time in my life are funny to look at as I resemble a ceramic doll.

I was their little doll until I was about five years old. Then my life would change forever. I was born at Brookdale Hospital in Brooklyn, and grew up in that borough. We lived a few blocks from the hospital until I was five years old. This neighborhood was a safe and friendly place where everyone knew one another and my family was well known. My uncle lived around the corner from us. In those days people with businesses on the main floor often had apartments above the stores, and we lived over a tailor's shop. I was allowed to walk around out front; the parents and storeowners would look out for all the children when they were outside playing.

One day I went to visit my uncle at his apartment. After my visit I began to walk home. As a child, I often played imaginary games, like walking on the lines of the sidewalk and pretending it was a tightrope. We didn't have electronics to blame daydreaming on. All we had were our imaginations. As I walked, careful to follow the line, dreaming about who knows what, I began to hear a lot of noise. It sounded like a huge car crash that with many cars hitting each other. As I turned to look, I came to an open parking spot. A car came through the opening and the car ran me down. *The bumper hit me in my face, knocked me down, and the car sat on top of me, bouncing up and down, until it came to a stop.* The only two things that kept the car elevated over the top of my body, and not completely crushing me, were a no parking sign and a parking meter. The car came to rest on top of those two things, with me trapped underneath.

The bumper pushed my lower jaw into my ear canals and caused me to become partially deaf. My right arm was lodged in the tire and brake system, and the sign and parking meter had held me down and pinned me under them, under the full weight of the car. Only a few inches between the car and my body kept me from being crushed. If the pipes had broken under the weight I would not be here today. God intervened, even then, to save my life. It is funny how this accident happened to me when I was five, and I can still remember the details quite vividly. The mind is an amazing organ in our bodies.

I heard the tailor and other storeowners yelling to "get the car off" me. They had a tow truck pull the car off me after they were able to free my arm from the tire area. Once the car was removed they all saw who was under the car and panic set in. Some were yelling for others to go get my parents; others were shouting to call for an ambulance. It was at this time a police officer who knew my father scooped me up and ran as fast as he could to the hospital down the block. The funny thing is his police car was running and close by, but he chose to run with me instead of driving me to the hospital. I guess traffic was heavy that day, or he was in a panic; it is still not clear to me why he ran.

In the Sixties we didn't have 911 (let alone cell phones). Most folks didn't have a phone in their home; they were a luxury not a necessity. Back then stores had phones with ten other people on the lines, and these were known as party lines. An operator would come on and ask us if we wanted to make a call and who would we like to talk to. Then the operator would plug us in to that line. If you needed someone you went to his or her house and knocked on the door. It was faster.

I remember being in the hospital on a table with big bright circular lights over me. I was terrified and crying—not to mention the pain was so intense . . . I never felt pain like that until this accident. The officer stayed with me until my father came in. Normal parents would hug and cuddle their battered child and tell them it would be "over soon." (There was some stroking of my head to comfort me.) After my mother and father came in and saw I was OK, I must have been crying too much; my father told me to stop crying. He saw crying as a sign of weakness. I guess it would have been a lot easier to stitch me up if my Father had let them give me medication for the pain. *He did not believe in drugs, so I received twenty-two stitches on my broken arm, and it was set and cast—all without any pain medication.* To say it was painful is an understatement. My mother, on the other hand, asked for all of the pain medications once my father walked out of the room, as she saw the horrific pain I was experiencing through this ordeal. My father had a high pain tolerance and he believed that fighting through the pain was the only way to deal with it. If you were going to a doctor it was because you thought you were dying. (My mother, by contrast, worked in a hospital and was so stressed out and suffered with migraines she took as many medications as she could to put up with what her life had become.)

My father wanted to find the person who had run me over and almost killed me. This was not a good thing, as anyone who knew my father in those days knew he was a strong and powerful man, not one to fool with. He would take you out in a heartbeat. But after a few days a knock at the door could turn his vengeance into forgiveness, and that was no easy feat for my father. The man who hit me was a friend, and I went to kindergarten with his children. So, what caused the accident? He had his brakes worked on earlier that day and had just picked up his car from the mechanic. The story goes that he had made the turn and stepped on the gas pedal to drive down the block. He pressed the brake pedal to slow down and realized his brakes had failed. This was a six-lane road, two coming and going on each side, and the other two lanes were divided truck lanes for delivery and public parking for the stores. He was bouncing off the cars and the cement trying to stop when he saw an open parking spot and dove into it. Only one problem: I was there at the wrong time, and when he dove in he hit the poles and me at the same time. He was so scared and heartbroken, as they were family friends, and more importantly, he didn't want to die because of something someone else failed to fix. I know my father talked to the mechanic, as he was the only one in town and a friend of the family as well. I was too young to know all of the details and what had happened to anyone.

Shortly after my accident, we moved to Dumont Avenue in East New York, Brooklyn, a place referred to by the neighborhood as "down the hole." We lived in a home in the neighborhood with an upstairs apartment, and we were comfortable there—until one fateful day. You see, the owner of the home had just painted the house and did not want my father to hook the clothesline back up to the window. This set my father off. In those days we did not have clothes dryers, like people do today; everyone had to hang their clothes outside to dry on lines. So this was a big deal, and my father had a fight with the landlord. Once he saw he was not going to win, he walked around the corner to view a piece of land, known in the neighborhood as "the hole of fame." It was for sale and my Father bought it. This neighborhood was built up to street level, but this spot was undeveloped and below street level and actually *was* a hole.

Excited, my father comes back to the apartment and tells us the wonderful news. We were to become homeowners, he said, and we should come look at where our new home was to be. In the Sixties you were considered well off if you had your own home or could build one from the ground up. We were so excited to go see the property. As we walked around the corner with my father, he could not contain his excitement. He took my mother and I to the edge of the dirt cliff and we were left to look down into this hole that had a shack on it. So my father had bought this hole of fame in this neighborhood. My mother and I burst into tears, thinking we were going to live under two pieces of plywood with a cement floor. But it should also be known that it was not unusual for my Father to build something from nothing. He was a master craftsman and car mechanic. It was said he had hands of gold and that anything he touched would turn out amazing.

My mother and I knew my father could build anything, but this was our first home built from the ground up. After he calmed us down, Father told us we would move in once the lower level was completed. Then he would build the rest of the house above us as we lived on the ground floor.

I was recruited to help, and so was my mother, until she was scheduled to work at the hospital down the block on Linden Boulevard. She escaped and left me to be the gopher for this project. In the beginning, it was fun. I would help set the forms for the walls and ceilings. *When I realized the walls of the foundation were being set so thick, I asked my father why.* The answer I was given was that if anyone tried to harm us, they would not get through the walls, floor, or ceiling. We had our own bomb shelter under our home!

There were two more levels to come. We spent 1965 to 1969 finishing this 13-room home that we all came to love. We had an in-ground pool in the front yard and I had an ice rink in the winter on the side of our house. Growing up, we had beautiful German shepherds, who were my friends, and a small toy poodle named Shotzie who would become my best friend. I loved this home; it was big enough to ride my Big Wheel through the rooms since we had an open floor plan that created a circle and my bedroom corridor was at the entrance to the main living area. In this home we always had company in and out day and night. I was the mini hostess for my father's crew.

I had only a few childhood friends due to my father being overprotective. Everyone knew my family and all feared my father except for the few who lived in the neighborhood and were approved for me to play and hang out with.

It all started here, where I went from being daddy's little girl to a tomboy who had to learn to sweat pipes, install the plumbing, and help wire our home for electricity. There was nothing being built or installed in this home that I did not touch. I learned so much during this time about construction. While we were building this house, I was not allowed outside to play, as there just were not enough hours in the day.

I have to say we did have what I call funny times. My Father dropped a steel I-beam on his big toe and hopped around, going *"ooh ooh ooh!"* To give you an idea of my father's toughness and personality, instead of going to the doctor he took a ten-penny nail and hammer and made a hole in his big toenail to let the blood escape to relieve the pain. My father had been an army medic, so there were no doctors for us.

Another incident was the ladder falling out from underneath him as he worked on the attic entrance to install the stairs to go up to that level. It was almost midnight when I heard my Father screaming my name; I ran out of my bedroom to see him hanging out of the attic opening over the stairs to go downstairs. His pain made me laugh because he made the funniest sounds when he got hurt.

Another funny story was when my mother and father once were in a heated battle. It was almost time for my mother to go to work, and I think she had had enough of arguing with him. We had sliders from the living room, which was the entrance to the home, before he added on a sunroom. As my mother went into the next room she shut the slider, being the clean freak that she was. The glass was clear as a bell and my father rushed to the entrance and did not know she had closed the glass door, and he hit his nose and face on the door. *I had to run into the bathroom and bury my head in the towel so he could not hear me laughing hysterically; he was madder than a hornet.* I did not want him to turn on me for laughing at his pain. To this day I can still see it happening and get a chuckle out of the memory. I know this is where my warped sense of humor comes from!

By the age of nine my mother had checked out from helping with the house project. She worked every hour she could at the hospital to get away from my father. It was during this time that their relationship fell apart. It started with verbal and physical fights over nearly everything. Most times the fights would burn themselves out if my mother had to go to work. If not, the arguments would last all night long and continue into the next day.

Grudges were the norm in our home, and sometimes my parents did not talk for weeks. I became their go-between and talked to each about the gripes of the other. I would have to be my mother's voice and tell my father everything she wanted him to know but wouldn't tell him herself. I did the same for my father until they would temporarily make up. I was the peacemaker, the one who tried to get each one to see the other's side. I was nine, so you can see how my life was starting out. Many times I would come in from outside to see just how violent they were being toward each other. Yelling, cursing, calling names . . . and then the physical violence would begin. My mother would fight my father back. She was not as strong as he was, but she would run her mouth and cut him down. He would become more violent and knock her down, but she would get back up. *She never knew when to shut up or stop antagonizing the beast that lived within my father.*

Twice in my life I was told to get my stuff because my mother was leaving my father. Each time we would run away, he would find us eventually. At other times she would run to work and leave me there to calm him down. It made no sense to me why we would run away to places like Long Island to live in apartments she had found for rent. He would always find us. This is where the old saying comes from: "There isn't a hole big enough in the world where you can hide, where he will not find you." His eyes, and his friends, were everywhere. He would find my mother and me and we would move back home. And for decades my mother blamed it all on me, telling me I was the reason she had to stay with my father.

The last time my mother took me and ran away and my father found us and took us back home, it all started to make sense to me. I began to understand my mother had not had a choice when she became pregnant with me; that meant a life with my father, married or not, because abortion wasn't allowed or even thought of in the Fifties. I was the last child my parents had, and the other children my father had with other women were not in his life anymore.

Maybe my birth meant something to him. To this day I don't know the truth.

The years in this home were difficult, but they also changed from day to day. One day we would be in chaos as arguments would last all day and into the night; the next day could be filled with love, fun, and laughter. I just never knew when I woke up each day what would spark a new issue.

I became a tomboy. I built go-carts and played handball and basketball. My father set up a hoop on the side of the building in our driveway. I rode my bike all over our neighborhood, which was about five blocks in size. I played with my dogs and did a lot of swimming in our pool in the summer; in winter, as I said, Father made me an ice rink to skate on.

But my father was also a jokester, and we would have fun together. As dark as life in this family could be, God was always placing his hope for a better tomorrow in me. My father did love me and thought he was doing the right thing in the way he raised me. He was raised the same way: "spare the rod, spoil the child" was the rule. *I survived, and today as I look back I am thank-*

ful to have had it hard so I could learn at a young age how to move through the hard times and overcome. God knew the lessons I was needing to learn to survive the hard times to come.

God sees what we are going to go through in life, and he plans for us to overcome. He gives us the strength to walk through it all.

Two

More Early Years in Brooklyn

Once I started school life changed forever. I was in a Catholic school from kindergarten to fifth grade, and the nuns, and most of the lay teachers, were flat-out mean. As if getting hit at home was not enough, I was hit and beaten by the nuns as well. They would say the "Our Father" prayer before class began. If anyone said or did something wrong after the prayer was finished, out came the wooden pointer that would smack our hands or hit us over the head. Erasers were thrown at children for chewing gum. If that didn't work, they would sit us in a corner in our undies with the gum on our noses until they felt our punishment was complete. Heads were banged into the blackboard, hair was pulled, ear pulling took place—you name it, the nuns did it.

There was fun in our school, though, and this came in the form of the bazaars and feasts the church and school had throughout the year. CYO camp was an event I always looked forward to in the summertime, as I would be in camp from 8 a.m. to 5 p.m. during the weekdays. *What a relief to go and be a kid and away from the drama for a while!* Security was provided by the mob, whose children were also in the school and church. We were all confirmed at the same time, so parties at each of our homes often consumed the days.

It was in kindergarten I was trained to fight because a boy who sat across from me in class was picking on me. He would kick my legs all day under the table we shared. One night I went home and told Father. When he saw my legs all black and blue he instructed me what to do to stop it. He trained me for battle over the weekend and told me if the boy kicked me again to get up, say nothing, walk over to him, and punch him as hard as I could in the mouth. I did just that—and broke his front teeth. I was now in trouble with Sister Mary Francis, who asked me who taught me to do that. I told her my father taught me to defend myself so I would not be picked on anymore. Of course, she called my father and asked him to come to school. And upon arrival my father promptly told her that if she would stop beating us long enough to protect us from each other, he would not have had to teach me to fight. Nothing more came of it except the boy who picked on me now carried my books home everyday, and we became good friends.

I learned to fight and stick up for myself during this time; it would become a deeply ingrained part of my life to fight for nearly everything. In those days Italian fathers groomed their daughters to cater to their husbands, to cook, clean, never complain, and do what we were told. I must have been made of a different caliber; those rules did not sit well with me. You can't teach a child to fight others to stop injustice and then want that child to be still when bad things happen in that child's own family.

So I reasoned that if being hit by others was wrong, why was it OK for me to be beaten by my parents? The answer wasn't long in coming! Strangers did not have the right to lay their hands on me, but as the child of my parents, *I was to learn the right way to grow up. Discipline and respect would be taught by any means necessary.* My mother and father were taught the same values from their parents and were raised in this way too. Here is another well-known saying my parents would often trot out: "If it was good for us, it will be good for you. You'll live." This just did not sit well for me—ever. But being young, what did I know? I had to shut up and do what I was told and be happy while doing it.

When we were at the homes of my father's friends I would sit on the couch in front of the TV. I was told not to move unless commanded otherwise. I had to wait for someone to ask if I wanted a drink or had to go to the bathroom. I was in no way to ask for anything from anyone—unless I was asked first. My father was all about respect. The old motto applied: see no evil, hear no evil, speak no evil. Tell no one anything about what you heard, even if you heard something horrible. "No questions, no asking" was the rule. In those days girls were to be seen and not heard. I never spoke without someone speaking to me first.

During my childhood, I was hit in the head with a metal vacuum cleaner attachment because my grades were not good, but this was because I was out of school for six months sick and had missed a lot of lessons and I was afraid of getting in trouble. So I made the decision to sign my mother's name on my report card. My scribbled signature must have been more than apparent since the teacher called one night after school to talk to my parents. The jig was up, and I was in for it. I was slapped so hard I was thrown through my screened bedroom window onto the landing where I hung our clothes outside my window. During other times I was dragged by my hair and handprints were left on my face from being slapped. I had black eyes in some of my elementary class pictures. This was the norm while growing up.

My mother was famous for the quick and accurate backhand to the mouth that always busted my lips from her rings. As I grew older mother liked to throw objects at me—and with dead-on accuracy. Her favorite were knives; I was told Sicilians love knives. Some would stay sticking out of the door of the room I ducked into as I closed the door before she hit me. There I would sit until my father came home to save me. One time I had to laugh. I was about eighteen and my Father came in and saw the butcher knife sticking out of their bedroom door. He turned to my mother and said, as he let me out of the bedroom where I had locked myself, "How many times have I told you not to throw knives at the kid?" I went to my room as they discussed what I had done.

My mother went through the change of life for ten years; her hormones raged and she became as brutal at times as my father. *Other times she could be as sweet as pie; my life was like a roller coaster, constantly changing from minute to minute.*

My parents were not always angry. It took something to set them off. Each had crazy triggers that would incite them to violence. Maybe it was someone shooting at my father, a stolen truck load of goods not going right, disrespect, or even not making a sandwich or cup of tea to his liking. The result would always be cursing, arguing, or a physical fight that would break out. On the other side of the coin, though, my father could be very loving, funny, and kind. He was the one to show love and kindness; even though he could be so brutal, he had all this love in his heart. He was like, as my mother put it, someone with a "Jekyll and Hyde personality." My mother also could be very loving and compassionate. When I was sick she always took care of me. We had a great relationship in the beginning. It wasn't until 1987 that our relationship went south, as my choices in husbands to that point had left her disappointed and upset. *I think she relived her mistakes in my life and resented me for it.* But truly, what chance did I have at a wonderful marriage with my parents as role models? I did not have a clue what a happy marriage looked like as most men in the mob had their wives and girlfriends on the side. The role models I had for marriage were cheating on their wives, lying, and never admitting their faults.

Growing up, we also had huge holiday parties with both sides of the family coming over for dinner to celebrate. Our home was a watering hole for, it seemed, nearly everyone. As rough as my parents were, they were loved by so many people who never knew of the violence going on behind closed doors. And if they did know, it was nobody's business, and no one would tell my father he was wrong.

We had many good times on road trips for the weekend to upstate New York to visit my mother's sister and her husband's family, who lived on an apple orchard farm. I would disappear into the orchard and eat wild berries and apples and play with the animals I would find along the way. These would be great times and most of my happy memories were made there.

My mother loved shopping for clothes and jewelry. I practically grew up in Macy's and JC Penney. To this day, I love to buy new clothes, shoes, and of course lots of sparkly jewelry as well.

Our family jeweler was a man named Andrew. He made one-of-a-kind pieces for us that my Mother would design. I loved going to his store, from childhood until after high school. I would go into Andrew's store in Canarsie because he had amazing jewelry from all over the world. *This is how I learned about buying love and affection. Every time my mother wanted me to keep her secrets she would take me shopping and out to eat.* It was always after a spree, and we would be relaxing at a restaurant, that she would go over the day and say, "Don't tell your father anything I told you." I would always agree. Who wouldn't? It was master manipulation at its best.

What did I know? I was a kid! When mom says, "Don't say anything to your Father" and, in the next sentence, "Let's go shopping," I didn't know it was to keep me quiet. But it was, and it wasn't until I was older that I saw this for what it was. I became resentful for having to keep lying to my father, but this was my life, and my parents were always right. I looked up to them as heroes. They protected me, taught me, and I went along until I started to develop my own mind. Then the truth becomes evident. What neither of us knew was that my father knew everything Mother did; he also knew when I was lying for her, and so sometimes I was in trouble and sometimes he would let it slide. He always knew her secrets; my mother thought she was getting over on him—and he let her think that unless it was a big issue, and then it was on. At that point, the battle for truth would rage until my mother confessed.

It was in our home in East New York where a family member was sexually abusive toward me. I was eight years old. No one knew what he was doing for a few years because he was family, and he told me I would get in trouble. In those days I did not want to get into trouble; I was scared as he was much older than me. I hated to go to his house to visit family if he was home, as it did not matter who was in the home.

One day when I was home sick from school, my father was passing by the living room window and he caught him in the act. *Finally, this horrible time in my life ended; I was 11. The only reason he was allowed to live was because he was family.* But he was never allowed around me anymore. This put a wedge between our families, and the shared holidays at both of our homes came to an end.

I had to put the pain of this in the back of my mind, as I did with all of the painful memories I went through. This boy was not allowed near me, and after some time I guess I just suppressed it. I did have more of an attitude toward others if I felt they were trying to hurt me; I would lash out first so they did not have the opportunity.

Forgiveness for this family member happened when I was in my forties as I went to visit my aunt with my sister. He was there to greet me at the car door as we arrived. He came to my open window and started to cry and ask for forgiveness. I was past it; I forgave him. I had to provide peace out of this horrible period in all of our lives, as not many even knew it happened. Family secrets were the norm. It was in my early fifties that I learned I was not the only one he did this to.

I grew up going to the beach from as far back as I can remember; I would go with my mother and her friends and their kids. Some of the beaches we spent time at: Jones, Rockaway, Long, and Manhattan. What fun we had during the early days! We would arrive in the early morning and be gone by 1 p.m. Mother was an early bird for sure.

These beaches were always my second home and my comfort zones. *To this day, if I have to live away from the ocean, I go nuts. I feel trapped.* So I've always lived by water. I find God's peace there—always. No matter what trouble or problems I would have, I would be at the beach, talking to God.

Three

God and Life in a Connected Family

I am so very thankful that I had the first few years of my life in Catholic school, as I met God there. No matter how dysfunctional the congregation was, I was introduced to God the Father and Mary the Mother of Jesus, the Son of God.

One thing I remember as a child going to church on Sundays was how many saints we had to pray to for help, when in fact Jesus is all we need. My family had the usual saints we prayed to for different issues, like animals, travels, and health. There were so many I could not remember them all, so I just memorized the Our Father and the Hail Mary; those were the go-to prayers I used when I was afraid or in need of reaching out to God for help when troubles came. No matter if we were good or bad, we were still sinners. *And I would always feel that there wasn't a way to ever be right in God's eyes.* It was a lot of pressure for me, as so much had been happening at home that was not in my control. Would I ever be able to do what I was told to do to be granted access to Heaven?

After fifth grade God was not part of our everyday lives. How could the church be so hypocritical, I wondered, with all that was happening around me? With all the lies, deceit, stealing, and loss of lives? *How could the people around me still go to church and ask the priest for forgiveness? Then the priests would grant it with penance and all would go on about their day; how could this be?* Much Mafia money was given to churches back in that day. Protection at bazaars and events was the norm.

This is where I became confused about the church and God's role in my life. With so much hatred and bitterness in my family it made me wonder if God even knew I was alive! I did not see him in our family. Once my Mother took me out of Catholic school after fifth grade, God was no longer part of my everyday life. I was then thrown into the public school system in one of the worst neighborhoods in Brooklyn. With no more church and so much death, destruction, and despair going on all around me, how could I possibly think God even cared about me or knew who I was?

As the family became more violent to one another and the world outside, fear and distrust were becoming stronger influences than the Lord. *All I had was my Sacred Heart statue of Jesus. I would talk to that statue since I had no one else to talk to.*

There are so many stories to tell of the verbal and physical abuse I suffered as a child. I hated my life and nearly everything in it. I vowed I would get out and never treat my child how my parents had treated me. As a child we need our parents to give us approval and acceptance. When you have a showing of affection and happy moments but then have to live with the knowledge that at any moment violence would burst out—and I would not see it coming . . well, I would go into my room and stay there until they were done fighting. I always felt such evil around me; I was afraid of the shadows and the monsters under my bed. Yes, I was always afraid when I went to bed at night, as I thought I could be pulled into hell from under my bed. From a child I would have these episodes of something coming from under my bed and paralyzing me. My eyes were open and tears would stream down my face; I could not move or scream! I could not see anything; I felt it holding me down. The only way I could get it to stop was to say in my mind, over and over, *Jesus help me,* and eventually it would stop. This happened continually, until I was 18. All through my life I have never had normal dreams. The only dreams I remember are those that came true: the warning types. My dreams included pets being hit by cars, fights we would be in—right down to the clothes worn in those fights—and friends who were going to be jumped. *I also had dreams of things to come concerning my father and family members I did not know.*

I now know these were prophetic dreams, a way the Lord would give me warnings to keep my family and myself safe, or even to change the destructive life path I was on so that the dreams would not come true. In some of these dreams I saw the deaths of loved ones. God was always warning me before it happened so I could escape. In the beginning I was afraid of these dreams, especially the ones that would reoccur for years to come. I still have these warning dreams, and I take heed to them even if I don't know what they mean. I am on guard and can see whatever is coming.

Looking back, I realize I've had the gift of prophecy from the age of five years old, when I had my first dream. One of my first dreams was during the Christmas holiday, and I had a dream that took place in a funeral home in which I saw my mother's family members all around and paying respect to someone who was in a casket. But I could not see his face. The next day we went to get my mother's mother for dinner. I kept asking to get the paper as soon as we arrived home so I could begin to go through the newspaper. I came to the obituaries and saw my mother's maiden name and asked her if she knew this person. It turned out it was a distant cousin of my mother's that I had never met.

And I had recurring dreams of horrible happenings. One dream I had as a young child was of myself, but much older; I was in a school setting I was unfamiliar with. As I walked into the school I saw lockers lining the walls; in one of the lockers there was a triangle vent in the top of door, and I saw a puppy's face through that vent. Even at a young age I was a protector of animals. I broke into the locker and rescued that puppy. I began to run down this long hallway and an elevator opened up and I pressed the up button, but it went *down*, and when the doors opened I saw the devil and all these beastly creatures. I hit the close button just before they got to me and the pup, and the doors did close and we began traveling up. When the doors opened I started running down the hallway and out the door and I woke up as I was running outside surrounded by a clear blue sky.

This dream stopped occurring when I was about 30. The battle for custody of my infant son was developing. I saw everything in these types of dreams as my fight for our lives.

My mother had a best friend named Mickey; they were two peas in a pod. She had three daughters and we would often hang out, all of us, to go to the beach, movies, and circuses. It was Mickey's children who introduced me to the occult. We had séances that had us scared to death, candles sliding across a table; the dead we called during a séance showed up late at night in the room we were sleeping in as the ceiling lights flashed on and off. All three of us ran upstairs that night scared silly! Ouija boards were the worst; we did not know what we were playing with. Let's just say no one should touch these boards, as they open up any spirit to come to you. Most of the time these spirits are very evil and hard to shake; these boards are definitely not for anyone who loves the Lord to dabble with. I learned the hard way.

Thank God for his protection; even when I did not have a relationship with him, I was still under his wings.

To this day, I do believe that the land my father built the house on in East New York was haunted with the souls dumped there from hits going on at the time. The area had been back-filled with dirt and then built up.

I was exposed to events when I should have been protected. I was told to get the gun when my Father needed it; he called it "the thing" and I would get it from his storage spot and bring it to him to take care of business. One event took place when he could not get the people in the projects newly built across the street from our house to stop throwing batteries, corncobs, bottles, cans—anything they had in their hands. These things were flung at our house and our pets below from their balconies. It was a seventeen-story complex of several buildings. It was a mini city: stores, schools, it had it all. Everything that was thrown was a missile with a mission: to whatever it hit below. My father became increasingly angry when my two dogs had cysts from the rocks and projectiles that were hitting them from above.

One night when he heard something hit the roof he knew where it was coming from. He knew the floor and he knew the balconies, so he grabbed his gun and shot the entire seventeenth floor of balconies in front of our home. Race wars had come to our house and neighborhood and my father was not playing their game. He would kill anyone if he had to to protect his family. After several altercations, a truce was made between my father and the tenants who lived above our home. This is how I lived—never knowing when trouble would come knocking. Most times it took a lot to get my Father to this point, but once the beast was out, all saw he was not to be fooled with as he had the strength of ten men, and he was fearless.

We never had any issues with the folks across the street after that incident.

My father was friends with most of the mob families as he grew up with most of them as kids when they came from the old country on ships to America. My father was an independent. He answered to no one; he operated on his own without payback or having to answer to the families. Stolen truckloads of goods and jobs my father's crew took part in were independent of the mob families' dealings. He had many friends and they knew my father's hot-headed temper, so they respected him. My father dabbled in the schemes that he wanted to participate in; he was not obligated. Shortly after our new house was built and we were fully rested, my father moved us to the country due to a load of goods he stole that had been stolen from him on route to our home. The mob familes were changing and the old-timers were dying, dead, or in jail. The younger crowd of mobsters who came in to take over had no loyalty or respect toward any of the old crews. Plus, after Gotti came in, my father said it was time to go, as there was no longer honor among thieves, and the feds were all over the Dapper Don after Big Paulie was hit.

We moved a lot. I was told we were moving for my mother to be closer to her jobs. Later I found out we kept moving so the feds would not know where we were. *Everyone I knew went on the lamb from time to time to disappear.* When times became hot and the police were cracking down, we moved again. In 1972 we moved from East New York, Brooklyn, to upstate New York. Talk about culture shock. Everything I was taught and had gathered on my own was no longer relevant. Everything was about to change.

We moved to Saugerties, New York and broke ground on six acres and began a new chapter in our lives. We were the labor—my mother and I—as my father cultivated a home out of a forest. He carved out a homestead, broke ground, and installed water, septic, electric, and a foundation for our home to be built on. Because the terrain was harsh, Father purchased a mobile home to put on the foundation as he built the rooms around us, and this became our home.

We lived in a home without running water as he built what he wanted on this land. I remember him showering in the rain in his Fruit of the Looms!, and I took baths in the stream across the road in my bathing suit. This spot was named the Devil's hole. The waterfall was beautiful and good for washing my hair. And I think this is where my love for animals came. I remember buying PH-balanced shampoo so I didn't hurt the fish; in retrospect, this is so funny. My mother worked at a hospital in Ellenville, so she was lucky to get a real shower when she went in early.

Once the home was finished, however, it was very comfortable. We were happy here and life was beginning to look up. My mother worked in the hospital about 40 miles away; she was happy with her job and life, being able to get out. She had to have action; she was an adrenalin junkie, so she worked in the ER or as ward clerk in different units. Her claim to fame started here; she was Operator 13, and this stuck with her in every hospital she worked at as a telephone operator. *All in all, I really thought we would be OK now. My parents were getting along, I had real friends, and I was enjoying the Catskills as my playground.* My parents' friends were all up here as well, so it was all so familiar.

I want to add a story here of what was a profound moment in my life. I would not know this was a turning point in my life until I accepted Jesus in

2009. It was at that point I began to hear from the Lord the answers to the questions I had been asking Him throughout my life.

It was soon after we moved to Saugerties, and I was 12 years old. I was bored as the town shut down at 6 p.m., except for the bars. My father had purchased a huge satellite dish so we could watch different shows on TV. One night I was watching TV in my room and turning the dial through the channels. (In Brooklyn we had four channels, but here, with the satellite dish, we had hundreds of TV channels from all over the world.) I stopped on a show that was talking about God. It was called "Praise the Lord with Paul and Jan Crouch." Everyone was so excited as they could just flip the switch and have a 24-hour-a-day Christian TV channel. They were funny and I kept watching, and as they said a prayer I said it with them. I knew I needed all the help I could get in my crazy world.

What I didn't know was the effect this would have all throughout my life. It wasn't until I started following Jesus (2009) that I found out this is when I said the sinner's prayer and asked Jesus into my life as my Lord and Savior. The prayer of an innocent and frightened child had been when God took me into his family—and He allowed me to survive my life. I didn't even have a clue I did this! But God did, and from this day forward he would protect me from the evil to come in my life and allow me to survive to accomplish his destiny in my life.

On the weekends, downtime for me was with my pets and the animals in the woods, as they became my friends: baby deer and squirrels all came to play. I would sit in the deer beds and wait for them to come. Everyone called me Dr. Doolittle because birds would fly into my hand, stay a minute, and fly off. I saved every injured animal I found on my adventures.

Behind our home property was a huge cornfield owned by a local produce farm. While out on my adventures, when I became hungry I would go eat the raw produce grown; this meant I didn't have to go home, and this started my love for raw veggies. A stream ran through our land, so I had water along with wild berries; I was out until it was time for dinner. I used to sit back there and daydream with Hunter Mountain as the background view that I was growing up with. Hunter was a ski resort and always very busy. In the summer, hiking was what we did for fun, but in winter we skied, snowmobiled, and would go sledding. It was always great fun.

I loved Saugerties Junior High School. I made friends, played sports, and was a twirler in parades. I was on the honor roll; I began realizing that school was not hard for me, and if I could get all my homework finished at school, I had time for sports and after-school activities.

But I started to get into trouble here as I was picked on constantly. Not only because my mother dressed me funny, but also because I was a city kid in their more rural area. All country people thought city people were mob, thieves, and whores. Maybe they were, but I wasn't. I had to fight my way through this school until I gained respect. Then they found out how nuts I was and soon left me alone.

I was a quiet child; I never started a fight. But if provoked, I would not back down either, because if I came home from a fight and lost, my father would send me back out to fight again until I won. Then I could come home and have dinner and receive all the praise from my father.

After all, I was my father's daughter, and people expected me to be tough. I had enough violence in my life, from infancy on up. All I wanted was to just make friends. But that was not to happen—until one day on my way home from school when a girl who lived down the road from me decided to start a fight and called me every name in the book. I was tough, and I did have a high tolerance for stupidity before my temper flared. I did not jump at the chance to fight. But after everyone on the bus joined her in taunting me, I snapped, jumped her, and began to beat her to a pulp. *After the window broke the beast in me was out and everyone was trying to pull me off of this girl!* We became good friends and hung out all the time.

I was kicked off that bus for a while, but I had made friends and earned everyone's respect. After the bus incident I was free from being picked on. Life finally became peaceful, and I was having fun for a change.

But after two years, we moved again.

Four

Life in Kerhonkson, New York

We moved to a place called Kerhonkson, New York. Now my mother was working at the Granite Hotel as a telephone operator and chambermaid. I was fourteen and coming to know my own mind. And what I was realizing was my father controlled me, and his thoughts were pushed on me on how I was to live and conduct myself in the world.

But I was also rebellious to that old adage: "Do as I say, not as I do." I was not fond of the idea of serving a husband in order to be a good wife. But here I was cooking and cleaning and always the one who sorted the loads that fell off the back of the truck. Mob life includes stolen goods that a few people (known as a crew) are in on stealing. After the load is stolen it goes to a warehouse or safe place to sort the truckload of stolen goods into piles for each crew member involved in the stealing. Being young and smart— plus I was my father's daughter and all knew I was trustworthy not to say anything of family business—I was the one who broke the goods up for the crew members to take and sell on their own. I thought this was a normal life; I didn't know any other way—until I was allowed to go to friends' homes and see how other people who were not in the "family" acted and treated each other. And then I began to realize how horrible my family was. It was in this home, in Kerhonkson, that I attempted suicide for the first time, and thankfully failed. I took pills and slept for two days. *When I woke up, I was still in hell and my parents were quite angry.*

This home we moved into next was a Jewish synagogue! So, essentially, we were moving into a church. As usual, my family lived in the kitchen as my father ripped the church apart and remodeled it for our new home. We were moving into God's house, and although I thought things would be calmer because it was the Lord's house, it was no different here. The fights and arguments never seemed to end.

But my father, as he always did, did a great job on the house. Soon I had a bedroom, and my father turned the attic into a place I could have my friends over to and hang out, a place that would not disturb my parents. I remember the first time I slept in my room. There was a closet between my room and my parents' rooms. My father could not bring himself to rip out this closet, since it was where the Jewish rabbis kept the holy vessels used for their ceremonies. So we used it to store blankets. As time went by I realized this was OK. Nothing came out of that closet to get me . . . I was thinking God could hear all that was going on in my home and that He would kill us for being bad. I had the wrong idea of how the Lord operated. What did I know? *I was dragged through this family aware of what they were doing—and it plagued my mind with guilt.*

As we settled into this area, I made new friends again. I started to work at the Granite Hotel, where I was a camp counselor and babysitter. And at dinnertime I took those goofy memory pictures people buy to remember their trip. I also worked at another hotel close by on my off time from school and the Granite; this place was called the Brook Hotel.

This is where new trouble began. I started to smoke cigarettes, and one day as we were at the indoor pool hanging out at the Brook, I didn't have a clue that my Father was spying on me from outside. (The pool had large floor-to-ceiling windows all around.) My friend gave me a cigarette, and as I put the match to the smoke we heard a knock on the window; it was my Father. He was very angry, to the point that I was scared to go home. I thought I was going to get the beating of my life, but all he said was that I was too young and it was not a good habit to pick up. He would not give me permission to smoke until I was eighteen. Wow that was it! That day I became a smoker behind their backs; my parents knew but never said anything.

Out of all of the hotels I worked in, the Brook by far was the most laid-back. One night after work a friend, who was a stoner, introduced me to pot for the first time. I was only fourteen. This night, when all of the kids were asleep and our jobs were finished, the girl I worked with took me aside and lit up a joint. After trying it, I thought I was going to die. I was so scared, as my mother had told me it was like heroin and I was never to try it.

Well, not only did I try it and live, now I had something new to help me escape. I became a pot smoker.

When I turned fifteen my mother felt I was getting into too much trouble working in the hospitality field, so she changed jobs and went to work at Ellenville Community Hospital in the cardiac ward as a data entry clerk for doctors and patients. My mother enjoyed working in the medical care profession, and it was here I became a nurse's aide. I was the youngest paid member in the hospital; it was not what you know but *who* you knew in those days that opened up doors. My mother's friend was the head nurse and began to train me to become a nurse, and that became what my heart was set on to be when I grew up.

I had twenty-two patients and did everything for them except administer meds. I cleaned and fed the patients and performed all the duties a nurse's aide would do. *I loved this job. It gave me a sense of worth, and the patients loved me because I made them laugh.*

During the week, I went to school from 7 a.m. to 3 p.m. and then to work at the hospital from 4 p.m. to midnight. I worked in both hotels on the weekends. *I realized when I went to work that I too was able to get away from being at home. I was turning into my mother.* She worked every hour she could so she would not be home with my father and me.

One night my father had a heart attack and was rushed to the hospital where my mother and I worked. He became my patient as I was on the schedule to work the cardiac unit that night. I quickly realized I was not going to be able to care for him because he would not let me bathe him or change his bedpan. My father was old-school: he never went out of his room with out a shirt on, never wore shorts, and never wore a hat in his house. He was taught this was disrespectful. So another nurse's aide was assigned to care for him. But after he was stabilized, he was getting out of bed too much. They attached a walking monitor so they could see his vitals as he walked around.

My father and his brothers had the strength of ten men. One time, building our home in East New York, I remember watching in amazement as my Father rolled a telephone pole onto his shoulder and ran off to get it out of the way so it wouldn't get run over by the heavy equipment being used!

I remember a story involving my Uncle Angelo, who owned a junkyard where all of the family went for parts when they needed anything to fix our cars. I was young at the time. As one the stories go , one day as my Father was fixing his car the jacks holding up the front end started to slip; the jacks were holding the chassis up so my Father could connect the engine to the car. As he was underneath putting it all together, both jacks gave out and the car fell on my father. He lay underneath the car, holding the engine off his chest with his hands, hoping it would not crush him! He started yelling for my uncle to help. Uncle Angelo heard him yelling and ran over, jumped onto the front of the car, under the hood, and as he reached in to grab the engine he lifted the block up off my Father and told him to get out from underneath. Angelo lifted it like it was not heavy at all! We were astonished at the strength of both of them. As I was growing up, everyone knew I had my father's superhuman strength—and in some ways I think this was what led to my demise. At a young age I could lift and carry items that were twice my weight and size—with ease.

So my Father made it through that first heart attack, another heart attack, and an aortic aneurysm. He was the original Iron Man! They would say that nothing but a silver bullet would take my father out.

I remember a time when my father's friends, who rode motorcycles, were on a run from Brooklyn to the Friar Tuck in the Catskills. They stopped at our house to eat, drink, and be merry. Guys were doing tricks on their bikes, and I remember one of them telling my dad to do "the eagle" on his bike. To my surprise, my father did it. There were so many bikers we could not see the end where they had parked. I have pictures of all the motorcycles lined up on our road in front of our house. After several hours it was time to get on their way. When they all fired up their engines, it sounded like continuous thunder, and as they began to ride off it was an amazing sight of a seemingly never-ending line of bikes going down the road.

I grew up riding on the back of an Indian motorcycle; that was my Father's mode of transportation. We would ride in the snow and rain. I don't think I minded a bit because I loved going really fast and racing. My mother had the car to go to work, so we had to use the motorcycle.

My father was a stock car racer, and an amature boxer when he was young, and his foot was always in fast mode. My mother would be screaming for him to slow down whenever he would drive us somewhere. I would just fall asleep in the back seat on long trips. At sixteen I learned to drive and I, in turn, became a racer and fast driver too.

It was in this home, in Kerhonkson, that I started to react like my father. One night, a drunk driver knocked over our mailbox. My father would not have been mad about it had the man just said he would fix it. However, the drunken man thought he was big and bad and approached my father. He asked my father what he was "going to do about it." It was then that I heard the magic words: "Go get the thing." "The thing" was his .357. *I had been told hundreds of times growing up to go get "the thing" when all hell was about to break loose.* I knew someone was about to be shot. So I figured I would get the rifle too. As I handed my Father the .357, I started shooting at the man with the rifle! My father was so proud that I had the guts to stand by his side and take care of business. He had taught me how to use a gun at a very young age, and I wasn't afraid of anything or anybody—just my Father. We were the talk of the mountains. His friends thought how awesome it was that his daughter stood by her father's side to take care of business, as if I was his sidekick.

After about a year and a half we moved again. The feds had found out my Father was living in Kerhonkson, and one day a detective called posing as a friend and asked me where my father was. Truthfully, I didn't think the code of never telling anyone anything when they said they were a friend. The detective showed up where my father was and informed him that I was the one who had let him know his location. When my father arrived home it was lecture time; he sat me down and told me if I ever told anyone again where he was when he was not home I would not live to see the next day.

So we moved back to Saugerties for a short time to throw the cops off the trail.

In the '70s there was a huge blackout in Brooklyn; my father and I went to get my grandmother and bring her to our home in Saugerties until the blackout was resolved. It was during this time my grandmother told us how horrible my uncle was treating her. She said he was stealing her belongings and leaving her alone and, with dementia, she would walk the streets not knowing where she was or where she lived. Luckily, she was a fixture in the neighborhood, as this is where my mother and her brothers and sister grew up as children once they were settled a few years after emigrating from Italy. Neighbors would find my grandmother wandering cluelessly and bring her home and care for her until a family member came to help.

My mother's mother was the last grandparent I had alive growing up; she lived in Canarsie. It was during this visit my parents realized she could not live alone, and they decided to move into her home to care for her.

So once again we were on the move. And this time, I would have no peace once we moved into my grandmother's home.

Five

Moving to Canarsie, New York

At the age of sixteen I was thrown into yet another culture shock. We were moving from the country back to the city. Living in my grandmother's house was going to be a very different life for me.

It was the summer of 1976 when we moved in. I remember having my sixteenth birthday in the basement of my grandmother's home. It was no sweet sixteen for me. I had a cake, blew out the candles, and called it a day. I always wondered why I never had the same parties or type of family that everyone else had. I was purposely kept naive to things and not allowed out past dark. I had to be home before the streetlights came on, as did everyone else. I was never told why we moved all of the time, at least not until much later in life.

All of the adults thought I didn't know what they were doing or saying as they always spoke Italian around me when they had their meetings. *I never let anyone know I could understand what they were saying because it could have landed me in big trouble.*

After moving in with my grandmother, my life became torture. My grandmother did not like my Father or me. I don't think she liked my mother, either, but nevertheless, we were the only ones who wanted to care for her. My parents lived in the finished basement and I was on the next level up in my grandmother's apartment. Her home had three levels. The top level was rented to a friend of the family after her son and his family moved out, and my grandmother's apartment was on the middle level. Life was hard here. She hated me. I was not allowed to touch the TV or open her refrigerator. Any chance she had to scare me to death, she would. She would not let me close the door to my bedroom. My grandmother's bedroom was directly across from mine, so we could see each other as we slept in our beds. When she started becoming increasingly ill, I would care for her and put warm towels on her legs for her phlebitis. She would tell me she did not like my parents, or me for that matter, and how her favorite grandchild was going to Italy with her. She would also tell me about the presents she would be getting for birthdays and how rotten my parents and I were.

I used to think, *How rotten can we be?* We were caring for her when not one of her other children wanted to be involved with any part of her care. We moved from the country, where I was happy, to live with her here in hell. It was here in this home that I started to have dreams of people dying and dreams of the devil. It was here I became afraid of the devil. One night I was awakened by my grandmother kicking my bed. When I opened my eyes she was standing over me with the most evil face I had ever seen. She loved to tell me: "Stop screaming. No one can hear you!" That's when I began to think that I must be in the wrong family. I must have been adopted. How can so many people hate me and still call me family?

Once my father had enough of the fighting and saw how I was being treated, he knew we had to go. I was very sick as a child. I had migraines, bleeding ulcers, colitis, a palpitating heart . . . and I was only sixteen! When I was born, they said I was super-sensitive and hypertensive. They were right; I could not handle the violence going on on a daily basis. And I had to keep it all inside as I did not have anyone to tell or to talk with.

I had to keep all of the anger and hate in my heart as I was being hit and thrown around the room, being bounced off walls for something I did or said wrong. If I tried to run, my father would grab my hair and throw me back into my room. I was trying to run away from him and his form of discipline.

Life was hard. I used to wonder if anyone ever heard my screams, because no one ever came to stop the torture. My mother was never home, as I have described; she would work around the clock just to stay away. The only thing that kept me going was my statue of Jesus, which I had until we moved from my grandmother's house. Did she take it and destroy it? I don't know, but it was all I had, along with the only two prayers I remembered from Catholic school days, the "Our Father" and "Hail Mary."

I would pray these prayers as I held the statue until the evil events would pass.

We moved out of my grandmother's house and into an apartment over a shoe store on Avenue L, next to the movie theater. For the most part, I loved it there. *Avenue L was always busy with people shopping, and I felt like I was in the middle of real life. I could watch how other families acted and how the kids were treated.* When I was punished and could not go out, I would sit by the window and watch as life passed by. I always felt like life was passing me by because I was never allowed to take part in any of the fun trips, go to parties, or attend school dances. I think it was the family who owned the store below our apartment, who we became family friends with, that finally convinced my father to let me go out with their daughter and her friends. I was 16. So now I was allowed to go and hang out in front of the house. I was allowed to go to the pizzeria and finally allowed to hang with the other kids in the game room. This was a place with music, dancing, and arcade games the owner opened for the neighborhood kids.

It was here I had my first fight in my new neighborhood. In those days you didn't talk about someone's mother and not wind up in a fight. I was the new kid, and this chubby blond kid decided he was going to tease me and call my parents and me names. That didn't end well for him. On the steps of the game room, in front of everyone, I punched him with all I had. I blackened his eye and, after banging his head off the steps, he ran with a new respect for the new kid on the block. No one bothered me after that; everyone knew I would fight at the drop of a hat, so I was not picked on after this incident.

The apartment over the shoe store was scary to live in for a different reason: it was infested with millions of roaches. As I slept I could feel them crawling over me and in my bed. I have never liked bugs to this day; it is not good if I find a bug in my home.

And I was still getting beatings when my father thought I did something wrong. On one occasion after moving into the apartment, my father couldn't find a certain photo album; he didn't believe me when I told him I didn't know where it was. He thought I was lying to him and knocked me around. Later he found the album in his bottom dresser draw and apologized for the beating, as he always did afterward. I always thought beating me to a bloody pulp and telling me he was sorry afterward . . . meant nothing. His form of discipline just never seemed to end.

After a year or so my father walked around the corner from the apartment over the shoe store where we lived and told us he had bought another "monster home," his term for all the houses he bought to renovate. This house was burned from the top floor to the basement. Once again, I was recruited to help clean up the rubble, but this time we were around where much of our family and friends lived, so they came to help my father and I was allowed to hang out with friends. The home was on 91st Street, between Avenues L and M, and my father had it finished in about six months. It was a great house, right in the middle of the neighborhood.

I felt like I finally belonged somewhere.

This home was a lot quieter; everyone had a place to run when the fighting started! My mother would go to work (of course), my father would run to the club, and I would be home—alone and peaceful. At this point, I actually thought they were getting along because the fighting had slowed down. But the secret they were keeping from me was that they were no longer together as a couple. My mother said she was sleeping on the couch because she wanted to watch TV after working all night, to relax before she went to sleep, and that she did not want to disturb my Father. In reality, their relationship was coming to an end.

What I didn't know was they were waiting for me to graduate from high school before they split. Not knowing of these intentions, I was happy for a change. I was allowed out, I had a few friends, and I tasted freedom for the first time in my life.

And I was allowed to make decisions for myself. Good or bad, they were all mine.

Six

High School Days

I started ninth grade at Canarsie High. After I did all the chores that I was expected to have finished, I was allowed to go hang with friends. First, I had to cook dinner, do the dishes, and finish my homework. I was allowed to go out until 9 p.m. during the week and 11 p.m. on weekends.

I was sixteen and still trapped in a violent world. My fathers' friends were some of the same guys you would see in a few movies you might be able to think of, and they visited our home often. The "family life" was evident in those days because everyone lived in or near this neighborhood, and they would hang out at the bars and restaurants close by. But at this point my father wasn't getting involved anymore with stolen loads; he was upset because of the drugs the mob was getting into with newer members of "the family." "There is no honor among thieves," he would say, and he would just choose to lay low. My family would go to parties at their homes and I was always inside their homes, watching TV; because of how strict my Father was, I was always the outsider and the geek in the crowd, the naïve type. As all of the adults were outside having a barbecue and a good time, I was a prisoner of my own life, not given any choices. At the time I had to do what I was told or face the consequences when we came home afterward.

I could go on forever telling horror stories of the events and times of my childhood, but *I think the picture has been clearly painted—we were not exactly the Cleavers.*

Every time I tried to take my own life by taking pills, somehow I always woke up. I could not even get killing myself right. My parents would yell at me for doing something so stupid, but nothing changed.

When I was admitted into the hospital— for pressure on my brain from all the blows to my head over the course of my life—my Father called me, told me I was a liar, and told me to stop looking for attention. Seriously! My brain was going to explode from the constant blows to my head, and in his world, all I am doing is making a big deal out of it? By now I was older and almost out of school, and I was looking to move out and have a real life. But what a joke that thought was, looking back now.

When the summer was over I started school again. It was here I met my best friend. To this day we have been friends, and that now spans forty years. Her name is Roseanne as well, although she spells her name slightly differently, as you can see, with an extra *e*. *Oh the fun and trouble the two Ros(e)annes got into! We met in speech class, and her life was as hard as mine.* She had to care for her entire family. We both shared a lot of abuse, and she was the one constant in my life, and has been to this day.

Roseanne was the one friend who stood up to my father when he tried to scare her away. He tried to chase her, but she didn't care; she was not walking away. She was as fearless as I was, and our friendship was started. It was also Roseanne who gathered our friends in the neighborhood to come to my house and beg my father to let me go out dancing and have a life.

It was at Canarsie High that the government decided to integrate our schools and began busing students from the really bad neighborhoods into our school zone. This led to a lot of fights between the kids in our zone and others. These kids were different; they were hoodlums bent on beating us up and stealing the jewelry off our necks and fingers. They fought dirty, with razor blades in their hair, and used knives, bats, chains, anything they could wield to bloody us and destroy our school. They roamed in gangs and preyed on those who were alone or weak.

We fought for equality; we fought for women's rights. (I guess what perplexes me now is how a nation of people that fought for everyone's rights in those days is just folding under the corrupt administration we have today.) By this time, I was known to be a fighter, and my friends would call me for help. *I would go kick butt, go back to class, or go home and have dinner. I was raised in a way that I had to fight for everything.* Nothing was ever handed to me for free.

In my junior year of high school I took steps to join the co-op program my school offered to those who were able to pass the required test. I was one of the lucky few. I went to school for two weeks and then to work for two weeks in New York City.

How amazing this was. I was able to go into New York City, the big city, for work. I was placed at a company called Morgan Guarantee and Trust on Wall Street, across from the New York Stock Exchange. The first few months went well. I took the L train from Canarsie into the city daily. The train went through some of the worst neighborhoods in Brooklyn.

One day while I was riding the L train back to Canarsie, I was standing by the door that led to the next car, hoping to find a seat. I was to get off at the last stop, which was Rockaway Parkway in Canarsie. This is when it happened; my first fight on the train. A group of thugs came on at 14th Street as we traveled home. I was in a short skirt and long maxi coat. I was watching them and knew what they were planning. They were staring at me as they were devising a plan to attack me. One guy walked over to me, sniffed me, and said, "Boy, doesn't this girl smell good." I knew if I did not strike first I would be in trouble; my father had taught me that.

They all stood up, walked over, and surrounded me. I started screaming at them to leave me alone. Then it happened. I became so angry I lost my cool, took off my high heels, and used them as weapons. I starting swinging and hit some in the eyes, some in the head. I don't know what else I did. I was so afraid that I instantly turned on survival mode, and then everything went black. Hands and feet were flying, and I landed a lot of holes in their heads as they ran off at the next stop. I don't really remember much of what happened after I saw black, but the results were there for me to see.

I experienced a few more incidents on the train and was dubbed "the crazy girl." This was fine by me. It made it easier going to and from work.

Seven

Starting to Work

During the years after high school graduation I continued to work in Manhattan. I had to fight off attempts at being raped, robbed, or mugged while walking to and from my jobs, and while waiting on the platforms for the train to come. It became so bad that I had to travel with a knife up my sleeve for protection. I remember a specific time as I was waiting at the 14th Street station platform to catch the train home. I found out later that night on the news that a girl was being raped behind the trash container at the time I was waiting for the train. So many emotions ran through my mind as I watched the news and saw where it happened. It was where I was standing. Could I have helped? If I had come earlier, would that have been me? I started to run scenarios in my mind of what I would do if attacked. My father always taught me to think ahead and plan for the unexpected so I would not be surprised if attacked. How horrible to have to live like this, but New York City was a hotbed of trouble through the Sixties, Seventies, and early Eighties.

I worked on Broad Street with a well-known telecommunications company for the U.S. watts lines. It was before computers, and we did all of the billing using huge ledger books. When my company moved to 51st and Broadway it became a fight to survive daily, plus now computers were being introduced, and we had to put all of the data from the books into the computers.

After two years I left that company and went to work at an optical manu-facturer as a telephone operator while using the old plug switchboards. The company was on 27th Street and 11th Avenue. A friend of my father's owned this company. He thought I would be safe working in a family orga-nization. I was, but I still had to get there daily by train, and I never knew what to expect when I entered the train station and boarded the train.

Another incident I remember happened after I began working at this busi-ness. It was a two-block walk from the train station. As I rounded the corner to my office I sensed something going on behind me. As I turned to look, a Hispanic man grabbed me. My first reaction was to punch this person with all I had. It was a total surprise to him when my one punch dropped him. When I looked back there were two guys coming behind him. When they saw him go down, I started screaming for these two to come get me. They saw how crazy I was and left. The only problem was that it all went down in front of my boss. What I didn't know is he called my father. He told my father what went down and suggested he get me a car so I would be safer. (My boss said I could park in the lot attached to the building.) This is when my driving to work everyday began. My BFF, Roseanne, and two other friends drove into the city with me.

We always had an adventure going in and coming home from work. One would think being in a car was safer than traveling by train . . . well, maybe not. Now instead of being underground waiting on a train in bad neighborhoods, I was driving through those neighborhoods, and now I was exposed to all the thugs on the streets. The difference was I had friends with me. Some of them were as crazy as I was, and they helped calm me down and kept me out of trouble.

I was 19 and totally out of control. I hung out with different gangs and cliques as most of my friends had boyfriends and were getting married. So I roamed New York by myself looking for something to do. I was very strong for a girl; I had inherited my father's families' strength, plus I worked out daily. I had to go into battle for my life on several occasions, and sometimes against multiple attackers, and always I would walk out. Roseanne said I would black out while fighting and, when I came to, bodies were laid out and we drove away. *I became known as "Batgirl" since I traveled with a bat and a few other weapons for security.* My father taught me how to use them, and off I went. I have so many stories, things like cab drivers cutting me off, my bumper being hooked by a city bus, being dragged down Madison Avenue, and more—but I will talk more about some of those incidents at a different time.

The point I am trying to make is that all the times I thought it was me doing the fighting, I realize now . . . it was God protecting me from serious harm. I thought I was tough because I could fight, but really God had my back. The Lord had plans for me that I did not know about.

I was a tomboy from the word go. I loved to race my father's car on the Rockaway Beach Bridge. I rode horses and ATVs and had no fear of getting hurt or killed.

Living in a connected family, there was nowhere I could go where my father's friends were not around and a part of things. My father knew everything I was doing on the streets; he was told of my antics. By now I would fight if I was touched or provoked. I never started the fights, but I never backed down, either.

In 1982, I went to work at a major trauma hospital in Crown Heights, New York. This was going from the frying pan into the fire. *Racial wars were the norm between the different cultures, religions and the people in the 'hood; each side desperately needed to learn to live together.* Cars would burn and gunshots rang out during the day. As if I needed an excuse to fight, I was also under attack by people who worked at the hospital. My mother knew the CEO of the hospital, and I landed a job in the blood bank. It was a city hospital, and all the serious trauma cases were brought to us since we were the biggest trauma center in the area at that time.

My mother worked as a telephone operator and was loved by all. But my mother never told anyone I was her daughter. She said I had to make my own way, plus I think she didn't want to be associated with me in case I would get into a fight or do something she disapproved of.

Cultures from all over the world worked at this hospital. I did not care about race or color, but others did, and they made it known I was not welcome. I ended up fighting my way through this stop in life as well. It all came to a head one day when my freshly painted Camaro was keyed; I had scratches on both sides of my car. I was so mad I was screaming around the buildings in the parking lot, yelling for those who did this to come out and face me instead of taking it out on my car. My mother was called and told to come get me; I was screaming in the area where three buildings came together. The jig was up, and now everyone knew I was her daughter. After that incident, and a couple of transfers, I ended up in the cytology lab as a transcriptionist for surgical pathology and the pediatric autopsy department.

I worked here for ten years, and I had to fight to survive during this time in my life as well. Most of these fights were because I was in the wrong place at the wrong time. Going out to lunch became a hazard, and I escaped being killed several times. I remember being out to lunch in the park across from the hospital with the guys from respiratory therapy. We came to the park each day to eat lunch and listen to music. Being a tomboy, I had more friends that were guys than girls where I worked. As we were eating lunch and listening to music, a fight broke out between two female drug dealers. At first we didn't think anything of it, as this was a normal occurrence here, but then it turned bad and we heard gunfire. The guys I was with started to run. They grabbed me and pulled me along. I was not as fast as they were, so they ended up carrying me as we jumped the fences to get away. I now know God was with me here, too, as some of the bullets either came whizzing by my head or, one time while going out to lunch, went over my head into the door jamb behind me as I ducked to get into a car. We think it's luck, or by our own power that we miss out on tragedy, but it's actually God sparing our lives with loving mercy.

You see, we go through our lives and conduct ourselves according to how we need to survive in the places we frequent. I guess people who have God in them know when He is there for them, but I did not. I thought it was all me, my strength, and my actions that kept me safe, that somehow it was due to my reputation of being a brutal fighter. I had yet to learn how much God had his hand in my life.

Everyone knew my father and being his daughter gave me extra street cred. He was always informed of my antics on the streets; his reputation was massive. Everyone knew he was crazy. The apple did not fall far from the tree. There was no place I could go, from Long Island to Manhattan, where my father would not be told by his friends every move that I made. I had no place to hide. It came to the point that my father sat me down and told me that if I were a boy he would not be worried about me, because I was always getting into and out of these deadly situations—as a girl. I did not care that I did not have any fear of those outside of my home; I feared my father, and he was the only person who scared me to death. I was always prepared for battle; every day I stepped out of my house I could face danger. My car was always my safety zone; this is where I carried my knife, a pointed screwdriver, and a few other weapons I felt comfortable with. I used them all to protect my friends and myself if we were out on the streets in some of the worst neighborhoods in Brooklyn and New York City. Roseanne was always with me, and we fought back to back many times.

After graduation my Father gave me more freedom, and Roseanne and I would go dancing every night, and some days we went straight to work from dancing all night long. I would show up at work in a leopard outfit or purple hair because we never made it home to change. We were into the punk rock phase of our lives. Roseanne worked at an even stuffier company than I did. She would not even be recognized as she strolled into the bathroom to change into normal attire. In those days, we drank a lot, played hard, and did a lot of drugs. I sometimes did not even remember how we made it home.

Once again, God was with me, as I never became addicted to any of it.

By the time I was twenty-two, all my friends were in serious relationships and getting married. I was now wandering all over, from Long Island to Manhattan, visiting different cliques and groups by myself.

It was at this point that I wanted to move out and be my own person, but my father did not believe an unmarried girl should be living on her own. He wanted me to be married before I moved out. I don't know how he expected me to get married when he chased all of the good ones away.

I still wonder what my life would have been like if I was allowed to date the only guy who came to the house to ask my father if he could date me. He was a good-looking young man from a great family. My father chased him off. I never had dates, or a boyfriend of any type, until I was twenty. There were too many threats from my father, I guess. I became a loner, frustrated and angry at my life, and I did not see hope or a way out.

Eight

My World Takes a Drastic Turn

This was also the time I was searching for my sister. No one had told me about her, and she was living close by. My uncle had passed from cancer. We were at the funeral home paying our respects. I was in the bathroom when two women came in and began talking about my father's daughter and how beautiful she was. At first I thought they were talking about me. When they said her name, I knew they weren't talking about me! And now I was on the hunt for my sister.

It seems she was a child from my father's teenage years before he went into the Army, and the entire family had covered it up. She knew of me, but I had no idea who she was. Because of the sensitive nature of this story, most of the details will be withheld. I will say that we finally did meet after my father passed in 1996. I had to wait for all parties to die before I could talk with her. While cleaning out my father's house to sell it, I found a phone number on a random pad and called it. It was my sister. We met and became fast friends. The family was not happy, but I did not care. They had kept us apart our entire lives.

In 1982 I was married to the only person who had ever asked me to wed. He too was a very abusive person. I did not care at the time. I thought love could change him; I was sure I could handle him. It was my ticket out of my parents' house. What I did not know was my life would be just as violent in my marriage as it had been in my home growing up. *Here I was, at this point in my life, protecting my friends from their abusive husbands, and I was marrying an abuser to get out of my own abusive house!* Because of his abusive ways, I didn't really love him as I should have when you marry it should be for life. Most of all, I just needed to get out and away from my father.

During the early days of dating, not one of my friends liked him because he treated me like dirt and was verbally abusive. But the truth is, I was this way also. He dished it out and I gave it back. He threw a knife at me one day and I chased him with a meat cleaver until I sliced his hand. I was aiming for his throat. Lucky for him, he put his hand up.

We traveled with his friends since my friends were all gone; this is typical for an abuser, to move you away from your family and friends. I knew he was this way from the beginning. He treated his mother so badly, and she was a very sweet woman and abused by his father as well. The funny thing is he was a twin; of course, I had picked the evil one. His brother was nothing like my husband or his father, but more like his mother, kind and loving.

When we were not fighting, we did have fun at times. We were quite active outdoors and traveled abroad a few times. We hiked and rode ATV trails; we loved being outdoors.

But all was about to change, and just two years after we were married. In 1984 I was hurt in an accident and became partially paralyzed. The pain was excruciating. And I had no use of my legs.

We moved into an apartment in my parents' house; we could no longer live in the apartment with his parents. The fights were too much for them. I thought I would be better off at my parents' upstairs apartment. My father did not work at this point and, if I needed him, he was just downstairs.

My first husband was always in and out of work, but during this time he was working. If I had a doctor's appointment my father had to carry me up and down the stairs. Our apartment was on one level, and I had to drag myself around when I had to do anything. Life was really hard, and I was now becoming a burden to my husband. He wasn't happy that I was hurt and could not walk. He became more abusive, if that was possible. He never came home, always working late. I was in and out of so many hospitals for traction, treatments, and all kinds of tests. If you can name it, I had it done. One test was a bone scan; I was in Mother Cabrini Hospital in New York City (no longer in existence today). They injected me with a dye called Technetium 99. I glowed for a few years! They told me not to become pregnant for two years to allow the dye to come out of my bones and system. My hair fell out. I did not know who or where I was. I had been in this hospital for a few days when my mother called to see how I was, and I did not know who they were, nor was I coherent enough to answer questions correctly.

On top of all this, I became very depressed. *I was always an independent person, and now I couldn't walk or care for myself.* Then, as if my health was not bad enough, my parents finally told me they were splitting up and my Father was moving back to our land in Saugerties, New York. My mother went and found herself an apartment close by. Then they dropped the bomb: they had never married. And if I had never been born, they would not have been together. So now I know why my mother would blame me for her having to be with my father. In reality, if they did not do the deed, I would not be here. So blaming the child is easier than admitting they made bad decisions in their lives.

So I was left to feel like all of my life had been a lie. All the wedding anniversary parties I had planned were all bogus: lies. Nothing they told me of their "marriage" had been true. My father had a previous marriage and a child with his previous wife. My mother had two previous marriages and left her children as well.

So now I had to move again, but now I could not help with the move. We moved into my husband's sister's upstairs apartment. More steps I could hardly get up and down. My husband was very cruel, and he would not help me at all.

He started to become more abusive, and now he had me all alone and I could not fight back. He told me several times he wished I were dead.

Nine

Beginning to Walk and Live Again

At this point, honestly, life seemed so horrible; I felt dead inside. My life was brutal, I was stuck in a horrible marriage, and my legs were not working fully. I was being verbally abused and having my hair pulled to get me out of bed.

The mother-in-law of a friend of my husband worked for a chiropractor. This doctor started me on my way back to walking, and without surgery. I believe this doctor was sent from God to help me walk again. He had hands of gold and his treatments were exactly what I needed to help me. I was not running the mile, but at least I was walking. After two years of being partially paralyzed, I was able to move on my own without help.

I worked hard to get back on my feet with hydro and physical therapy. Once I started to walk, my husband thought I needed a job to get out of the house, and so the hunt began for the right kind of work.

During my first marriage I suffered three miscarriages. I thought they were punishment for an abortion I had. This was many years before I was saved. Before then, the precious gift of life had little value to me. But after the abortion I experienced an aching guilt. This guilt of my actions has haunted me throughout my life. No one knew about the abortion except for my husband and my mother. If my father found out I was pregnant before I walked down the aisle, he would have been very angry. If my father found out that I killed this child because we were not married, he would have killed us both. Being pregnant out of wedlock was frowned upon in those days.

In truth, I believed all my miscarriages were punishment from God. I was always quite sick growing up. I later found out that I had a tilted, twisted, and inverted uterus. I was never supposed to be able to get pregnant. I killed the miracle I had growing inside. I did not appreciate life at that time. I was hardhearted and angry about my entire life, and I had a very short-fuse temper. Life was extremely hard.

After I began walking better, my husband found me a job with a mobster who sold wholesale flowers in the neighborhood market. I did the books and payroll, but also participated in their scams. I didn't have a choice; it was expected that I would participate.

After years of not accepting an offer from Roseanne to come get me and take me out for a night of freedom and to talk, I finally decided to call her and ask her to come get me. I needed a night out; we stayed out until 3 a.m. that night. And my husband was furious. I didn't ask him if I could go, let alone disappear for the entire evening, and he had no idea where I was. In the morning he woke me by pulling my hair and feet to drag me out of bed. It seems that the maid had come and put everything in the wrong place, and he wanted me to get up and fix it. I don't remember how long this went on that morning, but all of a sudden I flipped and the worm turned, so to speak. I became extremely violent. I jumped him, grabbed his throat, and was strangling him with all I had. This was the strength I had always had, since a young girl, coming out. As his eyes were popping and my nails were digging into his throat, I heard, in my spirit: *STOP! You do not want to go to prison for killing him, do you?* I snapped out of it and let him up. He went out and did not come back until later in the day. *I now know it was God who told me to stop. God was always there.* I thought it was my own thoughts that stopped me, since I didn't have a relationship with God, and I did not belong to a church. To be totally honest, I was wondering where God was while I was going through all of this. How could all of this happen to me? I was a good person, wasn't I? I thought I was. But in reality, my actions were way out there, and I didn't know the Father God, or who Jesus really was, at this point in my life.

One day after work as we prepared the table for dinner, the phone rang. It was my orthopedic doctor, who had performed several tests on my back to see if there was anything I could do to improve my condition. I was told there was nothing more they could do and that the improvement I had made was as good as it was going to get. No more activities outdoors. I was twenty-four, and I figured that my life as I knew it was over.

As I sat at the kitchen table with my husband, the phone call ended, and I told him what the doctor said. I expected compassion or sympathy, some sign of emotion regarding my issues. After all, this was my husband, who loved me, right? What happened next I never saw coming. As I got out of the chair and told him what the doctor had said, he hauled off and punched me in my right eye so hard I flew through the hallway, hit the wall, and slid down. He left me crumpled on the floor and then left.

My eye and cheek were all kinds of black and blue. I got myself up and made it to the bathroom. When I saw my face, I was enraged that this had happened. Now I wanted out, but how? I had no money and my folks were split on top of that.

I went to work the next day wearing my sunglasses. My boss told me to remove them, and none of my excuses were going to work. When I took off my sunglasses and he saw my face, he handed me $700 and told me to take the van and get my stuff out of my house while my husband was at work. I did just that. Suddenly, I was now sleeping in mob-run motels that had hourly guests. The beds at this motel had action going every hour, all 24 hours a day.

The funny thing is, once they found out who my father was, they put better sheets on my bed and tried to make it seem like a better place by putting mints on my pillow and turning my bed down at night! After I was on my own a few days, I was peaceful for the first time in my life. Even being at a very busy motel, I slept like a rock. Freed from my father and my husband, I was finally on my own.

My marriage to this man was annulled in 1985. I was starting over.

Before I left him I was on my way home with my mother from doing laundry. We were at the intersection a block away from my house. The light was green and I was not going fast as I lived on the next block. As I went through the green light a car that was doing 50 mph sped through the light hit us. The car hit us so hard the hood of my car flew up and came through the window, hitting my mother in the face. The entire front end of my car was now pushed to the right. I got out, adrenaline pumping, saw that my mother was conscious, and proceeded to yell at the crackhead that hit us. When I went up to his car and saw his eyes, I knew he was on drugs and flipped out. I grabbed him by the throat and began to choke him; in his panic he started to roll the window up. I barely got my hands out before it closed. In shock and with adrenaline pumping, I ran into the corner store to call an ambulance; I could not get my mother out of the car. Her door was stuck. As I lifted my arm to grab the phone, I passed out.

I woke up in the hospital between two guys with bullet holes in their butts. I had a busted collarbone, my jaw was out of alignment, I hurt a disc in my neck and upper back, and I had hurt my knee as well. My mother's jaw was hurt and her neck was wrenched. Here I was, finally getting better at this point in my life, and now this happened. Back to square one. This took me a few years to heal from. I would never be the same.

But once again I was realizing that God had to have intervened. As a habit, I had looked both ways, and I saw him coming and had a second to hit my brakes and turn the car to the right before he hit us. By acting quickly to turn, he hit my car in *front* of the driver's door instead of impacting my door and where I was sitting. If it hadn't turned out that way, I may not be here today.

Ten

Freedom and a Fresh Start

This period was the first time in my life I did not have someone ruling over me. No one was telling me what I could or could not do. I continued working for the flower market, and with only myself to support, I found an apartment and moved into it. I was happy; I finally had my own place and was on my own. I bought furniture from Italy. I loved to decorate my new apartment, and I made it my own. I was so elated that I had finally found my way on my own terms.

Life was good until my boss, who had a problem with drinking and gambling issues, thought his spot in the market was too small; he wanted us to move to a larger facility. He had me doing collections in the company truck. I would go out empty and came back with lots of brown paper bags with owed money in all of them. If the people who owed my boss money would not pay I would call him and he would send the boys out to pay them a visit. This was my job, plus the office work. So guess what? I was now under my boss's rule. He knew he had me where he wanted me, as I owed him for helping me when I needed to get away. It was a few weeks after I left that he started to abuse me sexually. I didn't have any choice because of who he was and the connections he had; no one would believe me anyway. This is the reason I never asked for help. In this version of the real world there are always strings attached or conditions to be met when someone helps you.

Once again, looking back now, I can see that God intervened here too. This is what provides faith to me today: while I couldn't see it then, I *now* see how God was working. Soon after my boss lost his warehouse office, we were selling flowers out of a trailer on West Side Drive in Manhattan. This was very close to the notorious Hell's Kitchen, a dangerous area to be in during the day and much worse at night. I had two guys who hung out in the trailer most days and nights, and sometimes I had to be alone until my boss arrived to relieve me for the night. It was dangerous and scary for me to be there overnight alone. Occasionally, one of the guys would sleep in the trailer as my bodyguard. In reality, my boss wanted him to protect the merchandise, not me.

There are so many stories that happened to me and my BFF Roseanne at this stage of my life. Every night was a new adventure of perverse and violent—if not potentially deadly—situations. We never knew what would unfold in front of our office trailer and flowers—and we had a front seat for it all. There were many times during this period that my life was in danger. We always think it is luck or by our strength that we get out of deadly situations. In reality, it is God saving us from ourselves and from the choices we make, as everything that happens impacts the plan God has for our future.

Left with flowers that needed care but no water, no light at night, and sometimes without shade, I had to get creative. I had an idea that I would climb down the utility shaft and plug the power cord in to the electric power plug so we could have light at night. My next mission was to get the flowers watered daily. After a visit from the local fire department, we asked for help, and they gave us a sprinkler nozzle and hose connection so we could keep the trees and flowers alive.

After losing the warehouse we lasted several months on this lot, and then my boss's drinking and gambling took it all away.

In the end, this gave me the opportunity to get away from the favor I owed him for his helping me get away from my ex-husband.

I went back to work at the hospital, but my back did not allow me to stay there long. In 1990 they released me from the hospital position due to being out sick too many days; I could not do the job. Some days the discs in my back would slip and, without surgery to fix the herniated discs my bones and vertebre were out of alignment, the pain was excruciating to the point that I could not get out of bed. I have to think stress had a lot to do with my back constantly going out. This was the last time I held a "real job."

At this point in my life, I was constantly in and out of hospitals and rehabilitation programs trying to improve my spinal issues.

My back issues plagued me throughout my life and would not allow me to keep a full-time job or any kind of steady work. It hurt too much and would leave my lower half useless. I couldn't handle it. I kept trying to work for many years after leaving the hospital job, but my back pain was so severe that it didn't allow me to keep the jobs I was able to get.

Without employment, I had lots of time on my hands. I was trying to do everything I could to get my back better and live a pain-free life. I would go out to Rockaway Beach to relax and swim to strengthen my muscles. I did this to build the strength my muscles needed to hold my spine and discs in place. The doctors told me that if my muscles were not very strong I would reach the point that I would not be able to walk. So being in the water made exercise easier.

One day at a time, and I had to hold on to hope that I would improve—if I didn't give up.

Eleven

Giving Love and Marriage Another Chance

After my divorce from my first husband, I tried to live a normal life. My goal was to be happy and find someone who loved me and didn't treat me like a servant or try to take advantage of me. My problem was I had no idea what a normal life was. I would see people around me who looked happy and normal, and I wasn't sure if this is what I was looking for or if they were just pretending to be normal. I thought I had an *idea* what a normal life was, but it always seemed out of my reach.

I never felt loved or wanted, so I was always searching for something or someone to fill the void I had in my heart. I so desperately wanted to belong somewhere; I was different and really never fit in. Having money doesn't bring real love or good friends. *I needed Jesus' love and infilling, but due to pride, ego, or just ignorance, it would be years before I would have this revelation.*

Then it happened one day at Rockaway Beach in 1987. I met my son's father. From this point on, I will call him Harry (not his real name). During the early days we had many good times. Harry was always good for a laugh. He had a good heart and was a great guy to hang out with. He had his rough patches, but he was always striving to do better. Harry, though, could just not seem to get ahead. During this time we spent a lot of time at Coney Island, riding the rides and ending up at Nathan's for the best hot dogs in the world. He played football and hockey and I enjoyed going to his games to see him play. His temper was intense, though, and he was always ready to rumble.

Harry moved into my apartment and we lived together until we were married two years later. But once again, this was not the wonderful, blissful marriage I had envisioned. He became comfortable and didn't look for work as much as when he had to live on his own, and our relationship became strained since I was the only one trying to support us. He enjoyed having his days free to go hang out with friends at the beach or catch a basketball game. Harry always had claims of not feeling well enough to go look for a job because he felt sick when he woke up in the morning. I am a compassionate person, and my theory is simple (and like that of most people). If you're sick, stay home and get better. But if you're sick in the morning and feel good enough in the afternoon to go hang out, you can go look for work. I guess not everyone has my drive; I worked through my illnesses and was raised to believe that it didn't matter how sick I felt. Work came first; I would have to be in the hospital for me to stay home from work sick. Supporting my family and keeping a roof over our heads always came first.

I will tell this part of my story and try not to portray Harry in a bad way. We are divorced, and I have forgiven him. However, he is the person he is; it is not up to me to change him. This belongs to the Lord. We made vows to each other: no lies, no abuse. I had been sure it would all work out without the daily violence I grew up with.

We lived in Canarsie, near Roseanne. Harry became friends with her husband and life rolled on; we had a lot of good times hanging out with them. I would cook a typical Italian Sunday dinner, and we would have good food and great friends to enjoy game day with.

After not being able to find a job, Harry decided that he wanted us to move to Pennsylvania for a job his brother's friend had a company he was willing to give Harry a job. I was dead-set against it. Our problems started when he could not hold a job. I felt that if he couldn't hold one in Brooklyn, what was so great about Pennsylvania? He said he had this great- paying job lined up, one with super benefits as well. Harry made it sound like this was the opportunity he needed, and it sounded good to everyone but me. My life was in Brooklyn. Everyone and everything I knew and loved was there. We almost broke up over it until my father, God love him, once again told me, "You follow your husband." My father thought my husband was trying to provide and finally grow up and become the man of the family. He believed he would take over and provide for his wife and future children.

Once again I went against my gut feeling and gave this move a chance. I was giving up everything to follow him to a place where his family lived but I knew no one. So in 1989, we packed up and moved to Pennsylvania, four hours from Brooklyn. Once again I was alone. I moved our stuff into the new apartment by myself; Harry had to go check in at work.

After two days of lifting boxes and climbing stairs, my back went out. I was in such pain that I was admitted to a rehabilitation center and stayed there for thirty days. I was put into traction to relieve the pressure off my sciatic nerve and from the herniated disc in my lower back. I had sciatic radiculoneuropathy, which means that my sciatic nerve was affected from my neck down; and my spine affected through my thoracic or mid-back down through my lumbar area, which is the lower base of the spine, to my left leg. This caused numbness and resulted in the loss of use of my legs. In my case, it had become debilitating, and I could not walk.

As I lay in the hospital alone, no one came to visit. I had to tell the staff I did not have family so they would let me do my own laundry from the wheelchair. My husband said he was always working late, and for an entire month he could not come in once to visit me. Roseanne called to check on me during this time. Finally, after crying to my mother and father, they banded together and came to visit me in Pennsylvania. When they showed up I was so happy. I finally had people who cared about me while I lived here in Pennsylvania. It wasn't until my mother and father came that I felt I could relax, sleep, and heal.

My father wouldn't let my husband get away with anything until I was discharged. Once I was released, my parents came to live with me until I was able to care for myself again. *Where is my husband?* I kept asking myself. *Why is he not here?* Was this the same person who promised in our vows to take care of me? He always claimed he was working to support us, but he couldn't take time off to visit and care for me.

It took some time, but I was finally able to move around, and my parents went home knowing I was getting better and able to care for myself. It was during this time that I found out through my husband's boss that Harry was not working late. He was at the bars with the boys while I lay in the hospital alone for almost an entire month until my parents showed up. The hospital's policy was not to let handicapped patients go home until care was set up, so when my parents came I was released to their care.

Throughout my life, to this point, I had always talked to God, but I never really knew if He was hearing my pleas for help. I didn't know how important having a relationship with his Son was. To me, God was always this far-away person who judged my sin harshly. As a Catholic growing up, we always talked to God; I prayed to Mary the Mother of Jesus. Mary is important in the Catholic Church as she is prayed to as an intercessor to God when we really need help. How backward that turned out to be. But I still had a few decades to go before I had God and Jesus in the proper perspective regarding relationships, and not just a religious perspective.

Harry and I started our lives in Pennsylvania once I was released from the hospital. I began to heal and I started to unpack the boxes that were there just before I got hurt.

I realized how alone I was even though I was married and we did the family dinner thing at Harry's parents and went out to dinner with friends. Something was missing, and I was so very lonely. *People ask: how can you be lonely when you are married? Simple: it's when one spouse is present in body but absent in mind and spirit.* Harry would come home late, eat dinner, take a shower, and go to bed. Even when we watched TV together, I was lonely. I knew he was hanging out after work; I knew the things he was doing because his boss told me everything. His boss was a decent guy, and he said he felt sorry for what I was dealing with.

To be fair, I have to say I was not the easiest person to live with. I had my own issues, my thoughts and dreams of how I wanted to live. I was stuck between who I was and who I thought I should be. God was working in me to change me, and I was fighting it all the way.

～

Because of my earlier choices and miscarriages, I had to deal with the truth that I might never be able to conceive. I did have guilt over this, and thought this was why I could not get pregnant—it had to be punishment from God. One day while I was showering I began to talk to God. *I asked Him if He would give me a child to love, one who would love me too. I needed and craved real love in my life.* I thought a child would bring that love to me; I had always loved and wanted a big family. I had always dreamed of being a mom and, at 29, I so badly wanted a child of my own. A few weeks went by and I was not feeling well. I went to the doctor and found out I was six weeks pregnant! The joy in my heart was enormous!

I was so happy with the life growing inside me that I danced around the house. I would put my headphones on my belly and play all kinds of music for my child to hear. I talked and sang songs to him. I was the healthiest and happiest I had ever been in my life. I now had someone to talk to, sing to, teach to be a good person, and give the life I never had. I always longed for a safe and loving home free of the drama I lived with in my family. I did not want my child to grow up in the "family" way; I wanted him (or her) to have all the opportunities I did not.

I envisioned settling down so my child could have lifelong friends and belong somewhere, so he would not feel like an outsider, as I had. I never felt secure since my parents moved so often through my young years, so I never had the chance to have lasting bonds with friends I met.

Carrying this child led me to start to change the way I thought. I became protective of the life growing inside me. I thought: *He will never be beaten, as I was.* There were so many delusions I had of the fairy tale life of love, peace, and security. I was so excited and could not wait until my bundle of joy would come home.

I was having a good pregnancy, not really having morning sickness. I thought this was going to be a breeze.

That was all until one day, while running for the phone, I fell. I was scared to death that I hurt the baby, so I went to the doctor to be checked out. *My baby was fine, he told me. I, on the other hand, was not.* The fall kinked my back and I started to retain water in a condition called toxemia. So from July to October, when my son was born, I had to take it easy and not exert myself. I swelled up to orca size: I went from a size 12 to a 22, and it became difficult to get around.

I was due to deliver in November. One day I received a phone call from Harry's boss. His boss told me my husband was going to be let go from his job. The only reason his boss kept him on so long was because I was due to have our child any day, and he wanted me to be insured for the birth and not incur hardships due to my husband being out of work. He asked me to schedule a C-section before the end of October, as he was stopping Harry's benefits as of November 1. My son was born October 30 of that year.

As I held my son for the first time, the families were arguing over such trivial stuff. All I knew was I would have to protect him from all the negativity in our families—and he was only hours old. I remember looking at my son for the first time. He was perfect in every way. He had strawberry blond hair and turquoise blue eyes. I could not stop kissing him and holding him. I would not let him out of my sight. They had to wait for me to pass out before they could take him to the nursery.

I saw him as the perfect child. He hardly cried and was so happy all of the time. I became a mother wolf, protecting him from everything around us. And he was my parents' first grandchild. They were totally taken and in love from the first day. *They were the happiest I had ever seen them as they held their grandbaby in their arms. I believe God gave me my son to help us all grow and soften our hearts.* My son taught us all to be kind, compassionate, and most of all, he taught me true love.

My parents came and stayed with us after my son's birth to help me care for my son and then to help us pack. Harry lost that job and now could not find work, so I started to search for an opportunity I could jump into to support our family. I was always the breadwinner; it's just how it was. After days of searching for a job that either Harry or I could do, I found a position in Haddon Heights, New Jersey. After the interview process, Harry and I were off to be community managers of a 20-unit senior complex full of loving senior tenants, folks who welcomed us with open arms.

We moved seventeen days after our son was born, and we started our new life in the manager's home. A two-bedroom house on the grounds of the senior citizens complex, it came with the position. The office was attached to the home, so I could be in the office and, with the door open, see all that was going on in my home. In the beginning Harry did the outdoor and other heavier work: landscaping, painting, and general maintenance on the apartments as needed, and when a new tenant would come in. (This only happened when someone passed away.) Most of the tenants had been there for many years and were more like family to each other than strangers. I really loved it here, and I was very happy to help when the tenants had issues. How gracious the Lord was to provide a safe home and all utilities (except for TV). All our needs were met.

But after a year Harry started to get comfortable and slacked off on the repairs. So I began to do all the repair work and apartment painting. At one point I had my son on my back in a carrier while I did the landscaping while Harry sat in the office and talked to the manager who worked in the office during the week.

After two years we were asked to leave, not because we were not doing a great job, but because the management was tired of watching me do all of the work at all hours of the day and night. At least this is the reason I was given. They hired another couple to do the job. Management had decided that from all of the reports they were given, Harry was not doing the job.

So there we were again, on the hunt for a place to live and a new job for Harry and myself. I found this great old house just a block away. I loved this big old house; it had a huge front porch, mahogany windows, and columns that separated the hall from the living room. Everything that was made of wood was mahogany. I could have lived there forever, but that was not to be. After we moved in and settled down, the hunt was on for work. I had always dreamed of having my own business, as I always felt I could do better on my own than working in a company doing the nine-to-five thing.

I saw an ad in the paper for contractors to become drivers for home appliance delivery. This was perfect: the pay was amazing and we even had the opportunity to purchase the delivery vehicle. I talked it over with Harry and asked my father to front the down payment; he agreed, and the next hurdle was securing the contract. I called the company and secured an appointment with the owner. This was very important, so I went with Harry to do the interview. This was not the time to let Harry go on his own, I reasoned; I wanted this gig. As the interview played out, the owner said he was willing to give us a shot not because of any great presentation of Harry's abilities, but because he felt secure with me running the truck customers and deliveries.

Harry was not happy with the owner's remarks, and I guess he could see through the man, as I could not. We became contractors for this home delivery company. This was a very lucrative business since we not only made money from the deliveries, but after finding a used appliance center to bring the old appliances to, we were now getting paid through two streams of income each week. I also took on a company that did corporate apartment furniture rentals; this business set up executive apartments for those who needed short-term living arrangements within the corporate arena. But with all of these commitments I became overwhelmed when Harry decided he did not want to work this hard. So he began to get comfortable and often became "sick" and I would have to hire guys to replace him as the driver or helper of the truck. I clearly saw the pattern he had developed; he would work hard for several weeks or months and then get hurt or sick and be out of work for weeks or months.

I ran the business all day as well as caring for our son. I was a stay-at-home mom and I set us up as a company. In many ways, we were on our way to securing our financial future and growing our business. All went well, we were able to pay off my father's loan to start the business, and we were making money.

But our little boy became very ill living in this beautiful old home, and we found out he had a severe allergy to mold spores in the old mahogany wood of this hundred-year-old structure. I was heartbroken as we looked for a new place to live once again. In our search we decided to buy our first home. The money was flowing in, so the hunt began for our own home. After a few weeks I found a sweet little house in Audubon, New Jersey, just one town over from where we had been living the past few years. I also started working as a waitress, 11 p.m. to 7 a.m. at the local diner near our home.

I loved this new home, and being a mom was amazing. To see my little boy so happy and full of love made me think of how we were raising him. Harry was harsh, rearing his son the way his family reared him. I knew I absolutely needed to break the cycle of violence of how *I* had been raised. Both Harry and I had been raised with the "family" mind-set; this had been a part of our lives since our youth.

And yet, still, God was working. He gave me the seed of love in my heart for this bundle of joy. My little boy softened my heart to want to change my way of thinking and acting so I would be a good example for him.

I began to have a relationship with God, at least in this sense: I was asking him to help me be a good mother and to teach me how to raise a happy, healthy child, as I knew my childhood had been far from that. *What we do for our children—sometimes these are the changes that save our own lives.* If we listen to the Holy Spirit's guidance, we will make it through.

With Harry claiming he was always sick, I had to hire someone to work for us on the days Harry wouldn't. I would be home when my son woke up in the morning. I would be there to take care of him and run the business until Harry came home from hanging out with the guys in the evening. He said he was working late. But I caught him a few times hanging out with friends, so who knew what was true? I lived on four hours of sleep a day. I was the go-getter and my husband wasn't; he didn't want to work that hard. We were not the same type of person. I wanted to retire early; he wanted to retire ASAP.

Harry would unload the old appliances we had acquired after delivering new appliances all day. Despite the problems, we were making very good money. Harry and the owner of the used appliance place became great friends, and it worked well all the way around—for awhile. But Harry would begin to hang out with the owner and the secretary and have a few cocktails to unwind; this was his reason for not coming home around 5 p.m. Usually he would show up around 8, or he would come home after work and run to the store with his friend, and I now had the friend's kids and my little boy until he came home. He was out partying; that was the bottom line, I liked to party too but I had responsibility and he became one too. I had to work at 11 and was not getting enough sleep; my body began to break down. Having a steady flow of income changed Harry. He came home late, never spent any time with us, and always left his friend's kids with me.

There were other problems. I came home three different times to find him passed out on the couch. Twice he almost burned the house down from leaving the tea kettle on the stove while heating water for tea; he would fall asleep as the kettle was on the stove. But God intervened, and thankfully no one was hurt.

Since I was not saved, I probably would have done something stupid to Harry if my son were injured due to his neglect. My son, now a toddler, would come out in the middle of the night to, I presume, wake his dad. When he could not wake his dad, my son would fall asleep on the dining room floor with his father on the couch. I would walk in at 7 a.m. and find my baby on the dining room rug asleep and his dad still asleep on the couch in the living room. This was our son! I had had three miscarriages, and I was not going to let my son get hurt or have anything happen to him when I was not home.

Imagine being at work around the corner from your house in the middle of the night and seeing fire trucks go by. You are left to wonder: *Are they headed to my house?*

One night I asked Harry to take me to the hospital. I am not the type to run to the doctor, so if I ask to be taken to the hospital, it is urgent. I was having excruciating pain in my stomach and I was urinating pure blood. I waited for him to come home to take me; his answer was that after his shower and shave we would go. So I drove myself and was in the emergency room; I couldn't wait for him. I was in the ER for more than eight hours. I had worked my body and mind so hard that my insides were falling apart. I had bleeding kidneys and blood in my bladder. I was told I had to take it slower from this day forward. I was on bed rest for two weeks. And then, back at it I went, as I could not rely on Harry to take care of us.

We started to work on the upstairs attic space to convert it into a two-bedroom area with a common TV area for both, with a bathroom for my parents to move in and help me out. Harry started to do the work, but this clearly was more than his capabilities could handle. I realized this one day when I came home and found a slump of compound on the floor as Harry had tried to fill a section of the wall which needed a small piece of sheet rock to close the new wall off. Instead, Harry decided to fill it with newspaper and cover it with five gallons of mud. Then he tried to install the andreson windows that crank out to open so the water would not come in. Well he installed the windows upside down; when it rained all the water poured in the open window. It was a mess. I just could not do the attic and work the business; with the care of our son, it was too much for me.

As I was working one night a customer came in to the diner and I asked him if he knew anyone who could fix a diesel Mercedes engine; our 26-foot business truck had been acting up. The dealer was charging us an arm and a leg for repairs.

I will call this man Fiske (not his real name) for my story. He came over to our house after my shift ended at 7 in the morning. I introduced him to my husband and they went to look at the truck. A few hours later the truck was fixed, and at no charge, Fiske said. So I figured I would ask him if he had carpentry skills. He told us he was a contractor and would look at the job to see if he could do it.

Harry and Fiske went upstairs to look at the work and bid the job. I went about my day; a few hours later he had hired Fiske to do the job.

My parents were both getting ready to move in with us. My father had his home and land up for sale. My mother was almost finished with her lease and was nearly ready to move in with us. Both were getting on in age, and I was all they had to care for them.

Obviously, I wasn't happy in our marriage. I felt betrayed after one time, in the middle of the night as I was working at the diner, a police officer came in and told me that Harry was in a car accident after leaving a local bar with a blonde woman. He was changing and I knew inside that something wasn't right. We were having arguments and some were scream-fests; this was something I did not want to do in front of our son. *I would flash back to my parents going at it, and all this made me start to think about divorce.*

I kept to myself with these thoughts; I did not want to make a move until I was absolutely sure in my heart this is what had to be done. I was not the only one involved; my choice would affect my son, and now my parents were changing their lives to move in with us. My son would be a statistic from yet another broken home. But I also began to believe a broken home was better than the vile words involved in our fights. They were becoming scary, and I was becoming fearful of the future.

I asked Harry to go to a marriage counselor with me, and he refused. According to his world, it was me, not him, who was bringing all the drama into our lives. I went to the counselor a few times, but with Harry not coming there was really no reason for me to continue; it takes two to make a marriage work.

The decision I had to make was for me to leave our new home and all I had in it, or to ask Harry to leave. After all, I ran the business and did what it took to keep all we had accomplished. I knew I could make it without his halfhearted participation in the business and our marriage. Most of all, he was not showing he could be the father I wanted for my son.

Meanwhile, work progressed on the attic bedrooms; things were at least coming together in that area. I would come home at 7 a.m. and go upstairs to see what work had been completed the night before. Not only was I hearing of Harry's antics while I worked overnight (from the police who came in the diner), but Fiske would tell me what was happening in our home while he worked upstairs. Fiske was from North Carolina, up visiting his daughter in our area for a while. Instead of Fiske traveling back and fourth from South Jersey, he would crash at our house during the night and start early back to work on the project.

But the truth was he was using our house to lay low, and using our remodeling job as cover while he was in town to complete a deal—a deal unknown to me at the time.

I began to get to know Fiske. He was engaged and was looking for land for after he and his fiancee were married. (He told me they wanted to move out of the city.) My father was selling his land in upstate New York, and I thought this could be a great match for Fiske. He could buy the land and, once the attic was finished, we would move my father out and he and his new bride would have a great place in the Catskill Mountains.

Fiske was always nice to me, always respectful. We would sit and talk about his life, my life, his upcoming marriage, the job and its completion—mostly small talk. Until . . . he told me my son was crawling up the stairs to get to where he was working! He said Harry would run to the store or wherever because he knew Fiske was upstairs. It became apparent my son and Fiske were becoming friends, and I think his hard heart was softening to the cute little guy. But truthfully, I was glad he told me this as I never would have thought Harry would just leave our son with a stranger for hours at a time.

During one of our fights I needed to get away and go home to see my father. I knew I would find solace for a time returning to the place I grew up in as a kid. Fiske wanted to see the land, and I needed a respite from Harry. And by this time my mother was already living with us as we were nearing the point of having all the repairs completed.

I told Harry I was riding up with Fiske to show him the land and see my father, who was busy tying up loose ends at his house to make the move. It was a good time, as I had the weekend off, so Fiske and I left for the three-hour drive. What I did not know was Harry was having a fit because I went alone with Fiske. I was not the one who couldn't be trusted, Harry was. After the weekend we came home. Fiske wanted to buy the land, and it seemed this was all going to work out and my father would sell his land to Fiske, move in with us and have cash in his pocket for the family. This was my fathers plan.

We arrived home about 10 p.m. and I went to sleep. The next day my mother, son, and I went to run errands. My mother had to bring her car to the dealer as she had purchased a new car and had an issue to fix. While at the dealership I took a phone call from Harry; he was furious and screaming at me over the trip. This argument was uncalled for, and I had done nothing wrong. Because of his guilt and jealousy, he was arguing with me. This is what started the ordeal that changed all of our lives forever.

Later, with Harry at home, and as a new fight was beginning, I asked my mother to take our son out of the house so he would not hear us at each other's throats, as it was about to become violent. She went to the park with my son, and a few hours later wanted to come home; I told her not to as it was still going on and getting worse. My mother knew how horrible this could be, so we made the decision for her to go to my father's house in upstate New York, where she and my son would be safe as all this unfolded.

During the fight Harry asked if I wanted a divorce and I said "YES!" It was one of those times where it just came out, and I did not know where it came from, but I had said it. Once I said that magic word Harry was so mad he turned around and came at me. By the grace of God, Fiske was coming down the stairs and stopped him. After hours of fighting, I wanted to go lay down and rest; my nerves were taking over and I was becoming sick. As a way to stop the fight, I went into our bedroom to lay down, but Harry came in and made me get out of bed. He said that if I wanted a divorce, I needed to leave. I stopped and said something like: "OK, let's think this out. I put the money down for the house, all of the furniture, and I paid for everything in our house." Most of it was bought by me before I met Harry, or my parents gave things to us as gifts. The car I had was new as I had just purchased it a few weeks earlier. Harry had a newer truck as well. And now I was being asked to leave. I didn't want to leave; he should leave. But he was out of control and my temper was out, and I was ready to get ferocious. As I began to get my son's things, and mine, I realized Harry was not letting me use my own car to load our stuff. I finally grabbed the phone to call a cab; Harry grabbed the phone out of my hand and told me to walk.

Fiske had been trying to be the mediator and defuse the situation, but Harry wouldn't calm down. I was glad Fiske was there, as Harry came for me several times and Fiske intervened. It was over and time to go.

I turned to Fiske and asked him to take my stuff and me out of my home; he had a pickup truck. Fiske clearly did not want to be involved in all of this, but it was too late for that by this time. He was involved, like it or not. I was pleading for him to help me get my stuff and me out of my house and away from all the drama. I took everything of my son's that I could carry and never thought to take all of my belongings, as I thought I could come back for them if we were truly splitting up. I had to leave everything I owned behind, except for some clothes and my jewelry.

I had lost it all again, as I was never allowed back into my home to get my personal stuff; it was now all his. I was furious and yet relieved at the same time. Harry's rope around my neck was finally off.

Or so I thought.

Fiske ended up having to drive me with all of my stuff in the back of his truck to my father's house in New York State. Shortly after arriving there, we unloaded the truck and Fiske left to go back to his home.

Anyone would think that if you and your husband have a blowout, give it a few days and it will blow over, or at least you can talk later about things. Not Harry. He called the police and told them I took my son and disappeared. During the two weeks I was at my father's house, Harry was calling my father to talk to him about the situation and to find out if my father knew anything. I didn't have family other than my parents to turn to for help, and though my husband knew that, he chose to tell the police he didn't know where I had taken our son. I wasn't home when he called so I don't know what was said.

This is where it all went downhill fast. A federal kidnapping warrant was issued against Fiske and myself.

I had no idea Harry had done this; I did not find this out until two weeks after I left. My parents and I were out on the porch talking all this over when my mother told me I needed to file for custody. I was so naïve; I thought that I gave birth to our son, so of course I would have custody. I was wrong. Not having a car, I called Fiske to come take me to the courthouse, and we left on August 17, 1993.

Reluctantly, Fiske had returned to my father's house, and he took me in my mothers car to Camden County Courthouse to file for custody on August 17, my birthday. Fiske knew I needed to be protected, and he decided to help me get this done. We drove down to New Jersey. I went into the courthouse to file papers.

As I was finishing up and I gave my papers to the clerk, she looked at me with the most frightened face I ever saw. She said that court was in session and I had lost custody. She told me of the warrant out for Fiske and myself and that I needed to leave quickly or I was going to jail. Further, she said, I was to hand my son over to the courts so he could be returned to Harry. There was no way I was handing over my son to Harry or anyone else; this was my child and he was staying with me. I know today it was a God thing, because she should not have told me all of that information and let me walk out of the courthouse knowing there was an active warrant against me.

I knew I had to walk slowly and calmly not to draw attention to myself. I was scared and shaking inside. I made it to the car; when Fiske looked at me he knew something horrible had happened. I told him to hurry and get us out of there. I told him what was going on and we drove calmly out of the parking lot. We were trying to get out of town. Now I found out my bank account was closed and Fiske's also was frozen, both due to the warrant. I was told that I had closed my account! This is when I knew that Harry had taken all of my money and closed the account. Fiske and I had to face the realization that we were stuck with each other until we could clear up this mess Harry had put us in.

I don't know what I was thinking, but I had a great fear of losing my son. I was crying, cursing, and screaming. "I lost my son! Oh God, why? What have you done to me? I was a good person!"

I laugh at this now as the realization sinks in that I was off my rocker just a tad.

We drove to a phone booth so I could make some calls and try to get a lawyer to help me. What a guy the father of my son was; Harry had left his son and his wife without a dime. It was after the lawyer told me that he wanted $5,000 as a retainer that my brain went into overload and I passed out. When I woke up in the truck with Fiske looking not so happy with me, he told me that because of his helping me his fiancée had broken off their engagement. So many lives were now ruined due to a choice I made out of anger and fear.

Fiske said that I was a weak person and after he was done with me I would be strong.

I had no idea what he meant, and I was angry he said that to me. I was a strong woman—or so I thought. I thought he was talking about my physical or mental strength. He knew I was not strong in the Lord; he knew I had great fear. *I had doubts when it came to God. I knew who God was and talked to Him all of the time, but I didn't know God could or would help me in this situation.*

So it was during this time that I decided to go on the run for our lives. I was going to break free of Harry and the "family" way of thinking and living.

I called Harry and told him I knew of the warrant and that now that he had done this to me, we were officially over. He wanted to nail me to the wall, and the threats began. But I asked if we could meet to talk things over, and he agreed. I was recording this conversation because of all the threats Harry was making if I did not give him our son. I set the time to meet him and started my way down to our house in New Jersey. I called him when I arrived—and a police officer answered. I knew Harry did not want to work anything out; he had lied. Now I had no reason to trust anything that came from his mouth.

Funny thing is, I still have the microcassette tapes I recorded of each phone call. I knew I could not trust him or the people helping him. I could only imagine what he told his family to make them believe him. He was the black sheep, always in and out of trouble. Why would they believe him now? But all were determined to keep funding him, as he needed money.

Harry lost the house we had purchased and all we had acquired from the businesses, which were going strong up to the time I left. I even gave him a couple of checks to pay the employees; I figured it might blow over as money was still coming in for Harry to keep it all going. But he lost the truck, too, which we had just paid off and needed to run the business. (It was worth $19,000.) He happily folded into the victim mode and drank and partied as he waited for the police to hang me and take my son. I know this as one of his girlfriends sent me an incriminating tape of illegal activity. How stupid Harry was while a battle over custody was going on. He wasn't upset or depressed in the video I saw. He was out for revenge—that was his driving force.

I left him, and his ego and pride were publicly hurt. Later events would prove all this to be true.

Twelve

On the Run

On the way back to my father's house, I called my parents and told them to get out and hide my son. Knowing how to live on the lamb, my mother and son went to a hotel under an alias name. They paid cash; they were safe for now. I had to think of my next move.

It was not the way I wanted to celebrate my birthday, but at least I was with my family and had my son with me. Fiske left to go home and get some clothes and money, and this is when he found the cops all over his North Carolina home. There was nowhere for him to hide, so he drove back up to my father's house in New York.

This is a day I remember very well, as Fiske proved to be not who or what I thought he was. He had a long past and was involved big-time with really bad people. Of course, this information would have been great to know when we hired him, but you don't exactly put that kind of thing on your resume. It was what it was, and I was lost for any solution to the whole situation.

Looking back now, I see how amazing it is that God sent Satan's soldier to protect me from the evil I was fighting! I had never been in this much trouble in my life, and I did not know what I had to do to keep hidden until I could figure out how to get out of this mess and keep custody of my son. *My parents were too old for this stuff, and I watched as it took its toll on all of us.*

The one thing I did know was I was not going to hand my son over to his father. He and I were not raised how I wanted to raise my son, and *I was determined to give my son a better life. I asked God to give him the life I always dreamed about.* Free from the wanna-be, mob-ruled mentality, a life filled with deceit and lies.

Shortly after we arrived back in New York, we had to come right back to New Jersey to secure a lawyer. After we could not get one to take the case, we were trying to reach a friend of Fiske's so we could rest and plan our next step.

But then, fear set in as cops came out of nowhere and pulled us over due to the warrant. Imagine my face when the officer told us the story that my husband had told police. I had become physically ill. I already had multiple health issues from stress. I was not in good shape to begin with, and I became physically ill on the side of the road. I was so pitiful, and now I had a date to answer the warrant before me. The date was set for September, and they let us go. Praise the Lord!

Being the person Fiske was, he knew we needed ID if we were going to be able to run. So we went to Elkton, Maryland and were married by a justice of the peace so we could have new identification. I was never so scared in my life. I thought we would be caught. After we had our new IDs we had to change the color of his bright red truck. It was a beautiful truck, and he loved it. He was not too happy about his situation, and he was really upset he had to paint his truck to help me out. We stopped at a park in a state forest he knew, and here he spray-painted his pretty red truck to black. Fiske and I could no longer come to New Jersey, so we drove back to my father's house in New York, where we explained everything to my parents.

Being my father was mob and Fiske was pure evil, they hatched a plan for us to go on the run with my son and my mother. Can you imagine ever being in this much trouble in your life, having this unfold because you love a child and want the best for him? I never loved anything in this world more than my baby.

Although I was not yet in a relationship with Jesus at this time, I continually talked to God. But I was also really confused over the whole God issue. Having been in the Catholic church, I was taught that no matter what I did I would always be a sinner. I truly believed that my son was a gift from God. I asked for a child and the Lord provided my son.

Throughout this journey, Fiske began to tell me of his theories; he was satanic. He knew all aspects of the dark side and said he wanted to teach me to be strong. I didn't have time to worry about Satan! I wanted to get out of trouble, clear our names, and get custody of my son.

As we were planning our escape, the relationship between Fiske and I became like sandpaper. We were both angry over the entire situation and how this was all affecting the people in our lives.

My father's driveway was about 350 feet long from where it began off the main road to the back, where the house I grew up in was on six cleared acres. The back of my father's land opened up to see Hunter Mountain in the distance. Fiske and I were sitting on the tailgate of his truck at the front of our driveway arguing over the whole situation, his losing his girl, becoming a fugitive, and not by his own doing, and the jobs that he had pending were left incomplete. The whole thing was like something you would only see with characters on television. The other people he was working for would be looking for him as well, as he never showed up to complete a deal he was in the middle of completing. The life Fiske had was a shock to me, as he had a whole other persona from the guy I met at the diner. He was a real bad dude, and I was now stuck with him to the end. I was so engulfed in the custody of my son, though, that I didn't care who or what Fiske did. After all, my family background wasn't very different growing up.

As our argument started to die down that evening, we heard a car coming around the bend. Anyone who has lived in the mountains knows you can hear cars coming for miles before they reach you. As the car came closer we heard it come to a stop in front of the wooded area of the property; we were about 100 feet to the left of where the car stopped. We heard the car door open and shut; next we heard the pitter patter of feet running into the woods. This started a modern-day version of the OK Corral. Fiske, who had more weapons hidden in his truck than I knew about, pulled out his gun, and we started to walk up the driveway toward my father's house to get my father. He was sitting on the front porch and had heard the car stop too. My father grabbed his pump-action shotgun and the two of them proceeded to blow up the woods the poor sucker had run into. As the bullets were flying, I began jumping up and down like a circus act to see who was in the woods and to see whether they had hit him. I heard the bullets whizzing by my ears as they ricocheted off trees. *I could have been killed here, and it did not faze me at all until after I was saved years later, when the Lord told me what a nut I was. If God did not love me I would not be here today.* He has shown me times in my life where I thought it was my effort getting me through it all, when truly it was the Lord saving me from what I was doing.

This is especially funny for me now as, while they were shooting anything moving in the woods, I turned and looked at my father and he was walking like he was limping. I start screaming to Fiske, "Stop! You shot my father!" Come to find out my father was walking up and down due to the waves in his blacktop from the floods we had there over the years washing the dirt out, causing the blacktop to sag in spots. We all started to laugh about the whole shootout; whatever or whoever ran in there either was dead or had crawled off our land. We did not care to look.

After this event Fiske and my father knew we needed the kind of help that could get us out of New York State. And since the warrant was out for Fiske, he now had to clear his name as well. Fiske decided to go to New Jersey to get the money and clothes left at his daughter's house. When he arrived around the corner from her house and saw it was under surveillance, and realized his New Jersey accounts were frozen, he had to get back to my father's house and go from there.

Thank God that in a savings account my father had the checks I had sent him to pay off the truck. We came together as a family, and the money that my father saved along with mother's money and credit cards—well, this is what we had to run with. Once back at my father's, we said our good-byes. With my mother and my son in her car, and Fiske and I in his newly painted black truck, we headed south, like Smokey and the Bandit running the chase car in front!

If the police spotted my mother, our plan was that we would cause a scene so they would chase us instead. We put my mother and son at different hotels while heading south, always under names Harry would not know. They would play grandma and grandson on vacation. He had all of his toys and electric car videos; he didn't know anything was wrong.

When my mother and son were safely hidden, Fiske and I drove from Canada to Virginia to look for a safe place to live. After eight feet of snow hit a town on the St. Lawrence River in New York State, we decided to go south! We found a great place in Lake Anna, Virginia, where we stayed until after the New Year. Fiske made a few stops in North Carolina, where he had money stashed. I did not ask or say a word about why or where.

Meanwhile, driving up and down the East Coast with Fiske, he started to show his bad side. This was as we planned to stay safe and out of sight until we had enough money for lawyers! We had lots of time on the road to talk and get to know each other. This is when I saw the other side of him, as he introduced me to the satanic way of his thoughts and actions. I was a fence runner, and had been disappointed by so many churches, where mobsters who would kill would go to confession and ask for forgiveness. I did not have the knowledge of who God really was, after all. *I had this rough life and only called on God in emergencies. And yet, it didn't seem like He was stopping the violence and hurt happening to me.* I loved his son in the statue I had as a child. But my knowledge of God and Jesus was limited to the Catechism and what I had learned while in Catholic school as a young child.

So, at the urging of Fiske, I read the satanic bible and the book of law. My thoughts on this as a religion were: *What a bunch of hooey.* The satanic bible is all about man being god and how we can take what we want. It's the direct opposite of all I was taught in those few years in Catholic school and church. And if I had not had that introduction as a young child, I don't think I would have ever known the Lord at all.

I was always looking for God; I just did not think He knew or *wanted to know* me. I was from a violent home and had done some awful things in my life. Why would He care about me? Besides, I thought I was a good person. I did not kill anyone. Oh yeah, I had an abortion. I tried to do the right thing, but I had been taught by a mob-minded family. *In truth, I was a good person by my standards, but not by God's. And yet, what did I know?*

Here is another time when God intervened. It was after the holidays on a beautiful day. I had this great idea to take my son and mother forty-five minutes away to the nearest town for ice cream. We drove to town in my mother's car, which was not yet on the radar of those searching for us. While in town we were sitting on the picnic table in front of the ice cream store and saw three police cars go by fast. They were in pursuit of someone. We ate our ice cream cones and left for home.

We arrived at home forty-five minutes later, and when Fiske opened the door he was white as a ghost and said, "Don't panic." When someone says don't panic and can stay calm. I wasn't the latter type; I panicked. Fiske told me the cops had found us and had my mother's license plate number, because we had just moved in, they where checking it out. In thirty minutes we were packed and on I-95 South following the big trucks. We followed this big tractor-trailer down to Florida, in the "rocking chair," as they call it. We traveled this way the entire way as a shield from the cops patrolling the interstate looking for us. It was like a movie and I was getting away with it all and keeping my son safe—or so I thought. Once again, we safely stashed my mother and son, this time at the home of a longtime friend of my family in Florida.

They both stayed there for a few months while Fiske and I looked for a new hideout.

After a few weeks of riding all over, we stopped in South Carolina in search of a house. We searched Charleston. Then we were back on the road driving around, looking for places to rent. We found a trailer in Moncks Corner, South Carolina. This was meant to be, as it was the last day, we had decided, that we were going to spend looking in South Carolina.

As we came to the intersection of 17A and College Park Road, I felt we needed to turn left, so Fiske turned left. As we drove, we came upon a mobile home sales center. I told Fiske to turn in; I had a feeling they would know a place to rent. I walked into the office and talked to the owner. I asked if he had a three-bedroom to rent that was affordable and he looked up, handed me a ring of keys, and said, "I have one I haven't put on the rental list. Go check it out." I walked out in a haze at what had just happened. After two weeks of running, I felt I was led here. We drove a short way down 17A toward Moncks Corner and turned into a small cul-de-sac with eight trailers. This trailer was large and fit my family's needs perfectly. We had been led to the perfect out-of-the-way spot.

And we stayed there for eighteen months—until we were found.

After we settled in and were safe and off the radar, I began to go over the events that had led to this decision to run. My actions were out of character for me; all I wanted to do was raise my son to be the best person he could be without all of the bad influences I had been raised around. With all the threats from Harry, and then him setting me up when I tried to meet and talk with him, I believed this decision to flee was the only choice I had.

We settled into this new trailer and then strange things started to happen that no one else saw—just Fiske and I. I think my mother *felt* the evil in our home, and she did not like Fiske's appearance and attitude.

Small, dark shadow figures could be seen running along the white walls during the day. At night, it was always a creepy atmosphere in and around the trailer.

Fiske built a fire pit in front of the trailer we were renting and kept a hearty fire blazing all hours of the day and night. He would be out in the yard by the pit, saying incantations, and the fire would blaze all by itself. It would burn in the heavy rain; it never went out. By this time Fiske was drinking heavily, and his sadistic side began to show its ugly head. He belonged to a biker club; no names will be used here. He regularly left to go meet with the club and would disappear for hours at a time.

I had no idea who or *what* he was. When we met he was in town to do a deal, and then all hell broke loose with my issues. Fiske was about six-foot-two;

he was built for trouble and very strong. And he was a Mensa member! He was extremely intelligent in every area of carpentry, electrical engineering, and a car and tractor-trailer mechanic. I don't think there was anything he did not know how to fix or build. He had a Mohawk with tattoos on each side of his head, and his arms had tattoos as well. When we walked into stores he was so scary-looking that people just moved away from him. I always walked behind a few paces to see the reaction on people's faces.

He thought it was funny to be able to turn off the streetlights as we drove by them. After we passed, the lights would come back on.

When you're in evil's presence and do not have a strong foundation in the Lord, evil will start to brainwash you with lies. It becomes a false, imaginary picture and one that is enticing to the lost. *I think of the time when Satan tempted Jesus. Jesus was strong in our Father-God. He could not be tempted. But I was a mixed-up, lost woman who was in so much trouble. I was trying to love the one thing I had that was pure and good and full of love—my son.*

But even after all that, after some time we appeared, to outsiders, to be a happy family. I enrolled my son in a Christian school under an assumed name; we had forged documents for his identification as well. My mother had so many names and IDs we didn't have to make one up for her! In truth, we were a scary family, and Fiske was the head of this house. Most people were confused as to why and how we came to be together. My mother my son and I were nothing like Fiske; we appeared normal to the outside world. We made friends who would hang out in front of our trailer around the fire every night, and Fiske would drink the night away. He could drink three cases of beer a day—maybe more if he started early. This was all new to me as during the past few months we were so amped up from being on the run that he did not have time to drink heavily. We always had to be on the lookout for signs of the police being on to us.

I didn't have the choice of letting Fiske go his way so I could go mine—not while we had this warrant on our heads. Our whole relationship was false because South Carolina would not let my son come home because he was living with us and we were not married. I did what I had to do to get my child back. We were under assumed names, married under false names and, truth be told, we could not stand each other. The heavy drinking started once we found a place to land for a while. He didn't attack us, but you could see the evil wanting to boil up in him through his eyes after a couple of cases of beer. He sure was big and scary to others. I knew I had to keep him in check for my family's sake.

But really, from having had so many men in my life who were more evil than good, Fiske was not scary to me. I did not run away from everything I knew to have this big, evil man hurt my son or me. My mother was on her own; she needed no protection. She would grab a knife or gun if he tried anything. My father had her covered, and she was as crazy as the rest of them, but she also truly loved my son. That was the only reason she agreed to help keep him safe while we figured a way out.

We lived on my jewelry, pawning a few pieces at a time to pay for all of our living expenses. We knew we had to have an income in order to accomplish our task and for me to be able to hire a lawyer to fight for custody in New Jersey.

After a few months Fiske and I started a pallet manufacturing company and sold new and reconditioned pallets to make money. This was a lucrative business back in the day. I was traveling to get my father in New York at the beginning of every month so I could bring him to South Carolina. He would stay until the new month's mail would come, and then we would drive him home to do his business and we'd drive back to South Carolina. We all worked at the private Christian school my son was in so we could be there in case someone spotted my son and we needed to run. We became members of that community, even doing chores for the school exterior. My mother worked in the school office from 1993 to 1995.

To some it may sound like a good time on the run was had by all, but in reality it was quite a different story. My mother had turned on me and was trying to convince my son she was his mother and *I* was his Nana! I was sick all the time from this family and my back issues were out of control. I took an anti-depressant medication, pain medication, and Fiske was getting drunk while entertaining the neighbors all of the time. Meantime, my father was always threatening to shoot someone over what I thought were stupid issues, but when, in his mind, he was being disrespected, the gun would come out. I think my entire family went out of their minds over this whole crazy time. I was never in this much trouble in my life. My parents were older and not quite on their games, but in their minds, they were still sharp as tacks. Most times the wars would start when my son was in school and be finished when we picked him up to come home, where all seemed to be happy.

I was tired of all the lies, my son was getting older and confused, and it was all coming to a head—and not in a good way. It was in 1995 that they were having a revival of Woodstock near where I grew up in New York State. My father was not happy about all of the traffic and people parking all over his land. He called and asked me to come to New York and bring him back with me.

While I was up there, he and I took a ride to the local store to get some food for the night. In our haste, as I put the groceries in the car, he pushed the cart away with my money, ID, and purse still in the basket. I did not even remember it being left there. We went to his house and it was then that I realized I had left it. We ran back to the store, but my things were gone. Someone had found them. I was hoping it was not in the store and they would run a check on my ID. I also had a large sum of money in the purse. Feeling uneasy, we left and came home. My father stayed home in case anyone came to the house looking for me or asking questions.

After coming home to South Carolina, I started to have wild dreams that SWAT was all over our house and up in trees with automatic weapons drawn as they came to get us. Fiske thought I was nuts, but I knew, even as a child growing up, that I never had normal dreams. They were always dreams of warning. Animals getting hit by a car if let out of the house, friends in casts, relatives I never knew passing away, or even fights I would get into in the future. *So after a week of these dreams I knew they were coming for me, and I began to think of places to hide my son.*

And then, one fateful day, on a hunch, the police did surround my house—just as it had been in my dreams.

The officer knocked on the door, my mother answered, and they asked her if she knew me and they showed a picture of me. She was angry with me at the time. She said yes, told them I was there, and invited them in for coffee. Fiske came in to my bedroom and woke me up, saying, "It's over. They're here." My life flashed before my eyes as they took me out of my bed in my pajamas, cuffed me, and put me in the patrol car. They would not let me tell my son what was happening. They were getting him ready to be put in foster care.

I was crushed that my mother gave me up since they did not know I was there; they had only been following a lead. After considerable begging to go to the bathroom—this was an excuse to talk to my son—I was taken back into the house and saw my son. I told him it would be OK and what was going to happen. He hugged me in my cuffs and watched as they led me to the patrol car.

He was taken by the department of social services and put in their car to be placed in foster care.

In my mother's head, she had a plan. She thought they would give her custody, but due to her yelling and tirades, they decided she was not fit to have the boy and took him away. *I will always remember my son's scared, longing eyes as the department of social services drove away with my son in the car without me.* I started crying from that time forward and did not stop until I was free and able to visit my son almost two months later.

When I was taken into custody it became a big story in South Carolina. I had no rights, and I had to be cleared of warrants and processed in federal court first, and then the state courts. After I arrived at Berkeley County Jail I told my story to the officer who had driven me from the county jail to the federal jail in downtown Charleston. I was scheduled to face the judge in my home district.

And the police believed me, as by this time they had known our family from living in the area for so long and had never suspected anything.

After I was processed the next morning, I would face the judge—and he was known, I was told, as the hanging judge. All I knew was I had to contact this judge and tell him why I did what I did. I knew running away was wrong, but faced with the circumstances and the actions of Harry, this had been my only option to keep my son safe and with me. The night before the hearing I wrote a ten-page letter detailing my entire situation and what had pushed me to do what I did. I was freaking out, wondering what was going on at my home with Fiske and my crazed mother. I was hoping they did not kill each other, or I would never get my son back! I had all these thoughts going through my mind. Would Fiske act and dress normal for the court appearance? Would my mother turn on me in front of everyone and vie for custody of my son? I had no idea what to expect the next day.

As I lay in jail that night, I played it all out in my mind. I was happy it was going to be over, but what would happen next? To me it seemed clear: For any chance to get my son home, I would have to take "The Addams Family" and somehow make it into "the Cleavers."

I was being led into the courtroom. Fiske was not allowed into the courtroom yet because a guard had let me talk to Fiske so I could catch up on what was about to go down in the courtroom. To my surprise he had a suit on and he was groomed! I was elated! He had his best side on display rather than his evil side that day—or I would have lost my son for sure.

Harry had flown in the night before, along with his lawyer. They were all set to take my son home with him after the hearing. By this time, my mother had been deemed unfit because of her actions. Fiske and some of my neighbors were in the courtroom to speak on my behalf. Strangers stood up for me as, once again, my mother had let me down.

This was the first time I had seen my son since being taken into custody; he was sitting on Fiske's lap during the hearing. Here was my little boy, now 5 years old at the time we were caught.

The courtroom was packed with lawyers and the press; this was a big story for this small town.

My father was in New York trying to get a flight out to come to South Carolina; he was waiting to find out how much bail money was needed for my release. I told him to stay home in New York because I was eventually going to end up in New Jersey. Fiske would call him along the way to let him know what happening.

It was time. I stepped into the courtroom and there they all were. Harry and his team—all there and all set to fry me. I was basically on my own, with a southern lawyer who did not believe anything I told him. My lawyer was obviously told lies, and he did nothing to help me. The judge told the court he had read my letter and he recommended my son stay in South Carolina until the court had more information on Harry and his capability to care for our son.

And then it was done. The judge had ruled. I was to go back to jail to await extradition to New Jersey. My son was going to foster care because the judge believed me. He did not want to put my son in any danger, either, and wanted a further investigation done before Harry was allowed to take my son out of state. We had ten days to prove my side. I stayed at Charleston County Detention Center and was faced with trying to prove my story at the same time. I was not allowed out of jail, as I was promised, because during my interrogation I was told by the detectives running my case to sign papers to finalize my South Carolina part of the arrest warrants. Not knowing what was going on or what the papers contained, I signed my extradition orders to be brought back to New Jersey to stand trial.

I have to say I was scared from the moment they put me in Charleston County Jail. I thought I was tough and maybe I once was. *At this point my heart was being ripped out of my chest, and I was scared and mad at the same time—not a good combination for me.* I wasn't scared so much for me as I was terrified for my son and what was happening to him. Charleston County Detention Center was no joke. These girls were crazy; they stole my food off my plate. I was getting pushed around quite a bit by an inmate in on murder, but after a display of temper I gained the inmates' respect and I was able to stay in the common area free of trouble.

I would go to Bible study on Wednesday to get out of my cell for a while. The food was horrid and I was becoming violently ill. The canteen was full of sugary food and that only made my illnesses worse. My nerves were getting to me, and I could do nothing to help myself; it all had to play out to the end.

Fiske would come to visit and catch me up on the happenings on the outside, including all of my mother's antics. He would even give me Scriptures to read! Praise the Lord! Even Satan's soldier was helping me find comfort in the Lord during the worst time in my life.

God stepped in and kept my son in South Carolina. My son went to a nice family. He was their first foster child. They took him to Disney on Ice shows. They took him on family dinners and trips. They took a liking to my son and treated him as family. Other than these few things, I had no idea what my son was going through at this home, but my fear was apparent.

Five days passed and then during a phone call from jail to my mother she thought it was a good idea to tell me that my son was being abused at the foster home because he fell and bumped his head on their fireplace while running. She was trying to drive me insane. She still thought they would give my son to her. She was way out of touch with reality; my mother was telling my lawyer to give custody to her because I was abusive and a neglectful mother to my son. Neighbors near where we lived sent character references of what they witnessed of my treatment of my son.

But after hearing my son was hurt, I lost my mind. I ripped the phones off the center bank of phones in the main area I went in to my cell ripping it apart. I was punching everything; my adrenaline was free-flowing. The problem was it was a cement cell! I was hurting myself, but it felt good to let out the anger I felt no pain until I calmed down and saw my hands all ripped up and swollen.

The guards were trying to get into the cell to put me in solitary. The inmates had heard my story and were trying to protect me, and once the inmates told the guards why I was upset they closed my cell door and let me wind myself out. Later I realized God had intervened once again. When do guards listen to inmates? It had to be God or I would have been locked in solitary until my extradition.

I had to clear my name and face the New Jersey courts that had issued the warrant to begin with. I had to have Fiske keep me safe from my husband, as he desperately wanted me in jail. He hoped to have my son forever, and hoped to see me rot in jail. I didn't want to go to New Jersey. I tried to have my case heard in South Carolina, but money was tight and lawyers were expensive.

Years later I called to thank the judge and found out it was his secretary who God led to read my letter. She had asked the judge to read it before the trial. The secretary told me that my letter was the only one in this judge's history that was actually important in his decision for a case. The secretary also told me she strongly believed that the Lord wanted her to get this letter in the judge's hand before the session began.

During the time I was in jail in South Carolina, Fiske brought me Scriptures to read. It reminded me of the time I passed out in the beginning of it all what Fiske had told me after he carried my passed-out body and put me in his truck. I remember hearing him say, "You're a weak person. After I get done with you, you'll be strong."

I remembered what he said then, and I knew I needed God's help for this one. I started to pray the only prayers I could remember, which were the "Our Father" and "Hail Mary." I started pleading for my son's life, for the help to get him back so he could grow up knowing God, and for the better life I had always dreamed of as a kid. When I was a child, I would get a beating for no apparent reason; I vowed to God and myself that if God let me have my son back, I would try to raise him in the Lord's way. I promised I would never deceive him again, and he would know how much I loved him. Honesty, trust, and love are all I had to offer my son. He would know and be a part of every decision we would make. I asked God to save us, and I would change myself to be a better mother and person for my son.

Late one night, around 10 p.m., officers came into my cell without any warning. They pulled me from my bunk and put me in belly chains and leg shackles. I started screaming and asking what was happening and why they were doing this. I had no clue what was happening. As the extradition officers were dragging me through the block, I yelled a phone number out to other inmates and asked them to call Fiske and tell him what was going on. Surprisingly, one of the other inmates did make the call to Fiske. Fiske called his connections to find out where they were taking me. He found out I was being extradited to New Jersey to stand trial. Meanwhile, I sat in the holding cell for a couple of hours as they processed my papers.

I was so stressed that I became sick and started bleeding from my mouth and rear due to my extreme nerves. I had to have a special diet and extra bathroom stops during this trip. As we took off from the jail in South Carolina, I found out that Fiske was following the bus to make sure I was OK—until they lost him in West Virginia. Although Fiske was a very dark and at times psychotic individual, he did keep us all safe. He stuck by my son and me and even took care of my mother at times while I was in jail, keeping her from getting arrested. (At one point she began shouting through a fence when she showed up at a safe house during a visitation Harry had with our son.) Fiske had a great affection for my son and treated him with kindness and love in the beginning. I believe it was the Lord who tamed this evil beast. As time went on I had to protect us all from Fiske, as his dark side was out there for the world to see after all of this was over.

I know God was involved as I look back at all the events that took place. I definitely believe there was special handling given me by the extradition officers.

As the journey to New Jersey headed out, I was being treated well for being a state fugitive. As well as I could have been, anyway, having been placed in belly and ankle chains and strapped into the only single-cell cage on the extradition bus that had made a stop in South Carolina just to pick me up. I thought at the time that *they* must have thought I was going to try to escape since they put me in a cage for the ride north to Camden County Jail. But now I know it was to keep me safe from the other inmates on the bus. I feared this was the mob using this as a ploy to get me out of jail and in a position that a hit would soon happen. Or was this the real feds taking me to trial? I was freaked out being in this cage on the bus. At first my mind was racing with crazy thoughts. It was really small and I was the only one in front in chains inside a cage. They were acting like I was an axe murderer or something worse, or that I could escape like Houdini from all the chains and this cage.

There were inmates from all over the country on this bus. It started picking up inmates from California and made many stops to drop off and pick up other inmates who had extradition orders from other states. The inmates were behind my cage along two benches, all handcuffed to these steel circles attaching their hands to the bench on either side of them. My cage was the front cage by the officers and the driver. I was still crying as the sun began to rise that first morning during the trip. We were coming over the Santee River Bridge. I was so scared and depressed because I still had no idea what was going to happen next—or what was happening to my son in South Carolina. Cheryl Pepsii Reilly came on the radio with a song called "Thanks for My Child." The words to that song made me sob and sob and sob. Once the song was over and, having seen my reaction to it, the officers asked me why I was there. I obviously was not a criminal. So I told them the whole story. Heck, we had four days to get to New Jersey because of all the stopping to pick up and deliver some of the worst criminals in the country.

It turns out the driver was also going through a horrible custody dispute and felt sorry for me. Being so stressed out about my son and everything going on, my diet needs were to have real food, not the slop usually fed to inmates on this run. We had coffee in the morning and food from Mc-Donald's and stopped for frequent bathroom breaks— all because of me. The officers would stop if I asked. The inmates would ask me to request something like a bathroom stop, food, or cigarette breaks. It was gross and horrible to travel hundreds of miles reeking of urine.

After the officers began to get to know me, they let my hands go uncuffed for the ride. *God had softened the extradition officers' hearts toward me and I began to relax enough to calm down a bit.*

During the four-day trip north to New Jersey we had to stop and stay overnight in some of the worst prisons I have ever seen. During my young life all of the mobsters had called going to jail "going to college." The Maryland House of Detention stands out in my mind because of all the horrible stories we heard about. This was a long-term facility housing some of the most vicious criminals. This place was different than the others. We weren't allowed off the bus as we only stopped to drop off one inmate and pick up another for drop-off down the road.

We could see through the bus windows while loading and unloading prisoners. They had televisions in their cells, stoves, small refrigerators with food, and laundry hanging near open windows. These inmates did not seem to mind being there. This was a massive facility and I had the feeling of being on the edge of an eruption into violence at any moment. The yards were full of inmates yelling at each other and taunting us on the bus. I was happy to be in a cage this time! The other jails we stopped at did not allow all the amenities we saw at the Maryland prison.

And then it became really scary when the inmates on the bus began talking of overtaking the guards and making a run for it. I worried if they would actually try to do it. Would they kill me too? Worse yet, leave me in the bus to die if they could get the vehicle to crash in the water, as some were talking of doing? Hearing all this crazy talk while cuffed to a bench in a cage didn't help my nerves or my thoughts. What would happen to my son if I died? All I could think about was my son and whether I was going to be killed.

After some time of being on the road I was able to get some sleep. When I woke up I noticed we were in Pennsylvania. I recognized the neighborhood. We were blocks away from my husband's family's homes! I went into a panic, not knowing if a hit would happen when we stopped for a bathroom and food break before getting into New Jersey. I saw where we were and started telling the officers we should not be here. If they knew I was on the bus, I knew, they could try to kill me. As Harry told me over and over again, if they were given the chance or opportunity, they would do so. We still had to make a stop, but everyone did what they needed to do at this quick mart kind of place, and then they loaded us back into our cages or shackles and on we went to New Jersey. I was shaking like a leaf and looking around the whole time, just waiting for something to happen.

Once we were on our way again, I thought the hit was happening because all of a sudden a loud explosion that sounded like a gunshot went off and we were all sprayed with what we thought was blood. The driver started swerving all over the road. He didn't know if he was bleeding or just felt liquid on him. The inmates were screaming and cursing to get me off the bus before they all got killed on account of me. All was in complete chaos. I was screaming, "I told you so! They are going to try to kill me!" We finally pulled over and stopped to check what had happened and if anyone had been shot. And what was on us? Not blood like we all thought. It was a can of Coke that exploded and sprayed us all. After figuring out what caused the explosion, all the inmates and officers starting laughing hysterically for a few minutes. After we gained our composure the driver was able to head out again. What a bunch of crybabies they were, all screaming to get me off the bus before they got killed because of me. I had been thinking they were so tough, and I was laughing so hard I was glad we stopped for the bathroom again!

I want to take this break from my story to say that even though I did not know God at this point, He was with me and helped me through this whole ordeal. From the way the officers took care of me in the South Carolina jails to the officers on the bus cutting me slack for food and bathroom breaks and unlocking my hands and putting me in the cage to protect me from the other inmates while on the bus—all of this was God's protection.

It was not until we reached New Jersey that everything went bad, and fast. *But God knew what was to come and, as always, He was several steps ahead of me.*

Little did I know then that God would once again rescue me and pull me through.

Thirteen

Facing the Charges in
Camden County, New Jersey

We crossed the border from Pennsylvania into New Jersey and were getting closer to the jail when an unmarked car pulled up alongside the bus and asked if I was on it. The officers told them I was.

I started yelling at the officers. "Why would they ask for me? Do you know who they are? Are they cops or the mob?" *Why would they tell them yes?* I was freaking out not knowing who they were and which side the men were on—mine or the mob. Thank God it turned out they knew Fiske, and he was on his way from South Carolina to New Jersey. They were making sure I was alive and on the bus as there were many other buses coming in that day from all over the country.

We finally arrived at Camden County Jail and the local officers were very angry that they had been forced to chase me all over the east coast. I was tossed in a cell for eleven hours without a bathroom break, food, or a drink as I sat in booking.

I asked to make a phone call. I had no rights at this point. I was a fugitive of the state and they had just bagged me on a kidnapping charge. So I was guilty in their eyes, and they were determined to make me pay for it.

The prisoner-processing experience is something I never want to experience again. I was taken into a shower area where I was stripped and cavity-searched for weapons. I had come from another jail and had been on a bus for four days; where would I get anything to hide? For their enjoyment they made me jump up and down naked while they all laughed. I was so humiliated and out of my mind with fear of what they would do to me next. The only thing that kept me in control was staying focused on getting out and getting my son back. *He was worth it all. I would survive this and live through it just to get him back safe.*

They took blood for drugs and STDs and threw me back into the cell in my orange jumpsuit, where I sat for what seemed like hours. Then they gave me a roll of lumpy material to use as a bed, and they gave me back my cigarettes and matches. I was once again put in shackles and belly chains and walked up and down hallways to elevators, carrying my clothes and bed roll, until we arrived at my new home—so to speak—another pod of cells. There was a metal walkway and a pod for the corrections officers in the middle. On one side was a door with a pod of cells inside it; each cell held two people. There was a total of four cells in this pod, and these were solitary containment cells. This is where we would stay for ten days in case we had any diseases. It was our incubation period, to make sure we did not have anything contagious before they put us in the general population pod with all the other inmates.

I had a corner cell next to the general population pod. I could see in their window—and it was not good. I watched as they had fights using a toothbrush made into a knife. I saw the officers go in and lock the area down from fights. This jail was no joke. This was the real deal, and I wanted out before I had to go in there. I was lucky Fiske had handed me cigarettes and matches before I went into processing. (You were still allowed to smoke in jail in those days.) He knew it would give me something to barter with the other inmates so they did not kick my butt. I learned how to split a match into four matches so they could light their cigarettes. I was alone until they put another girl in with me. She was kind to me as she had been in this jail before, and she began to school me on how to stay safe in the general population. It did not look like I was getting out anytime soon. The guards watched us at all times, even as we showered; they liked looking at the naked women as they showered. This was the only time we were allowed out of the cell.

After nine days of being in this jail I was told I had a trial date in two days. I would not be put in the general population until after my trial.

The day finally came for me to go to trial, and I was crying the entire time. On every jail cell I was in I wrote "God help me"—and I also wrote my son's name on the wall.

When the time came for me to go to court, I was hooked to a bunch of men and placed at the end of the line as we made our way to the court building. I guess the guards were talking about my case because the guys started calling out to me, saying, "Hang tough, white bread, you'll be OK." I was crying so much fear had taken over my entire body; I was shaking uncontrollably. And then the time finally arrived. Would it all end or would I end up in prison? What would happen to my son if I were found guilty? What if his father won custody? All I could think of was getting out of jail, getting my name cleared, and being able to see my son. *It was close to two months since I last saw him and we had never been apart before this all started.* After being in a holding cell for what seemed like hours, I was called into the courtroom. I was still crying as I was led into the courtroom, and then I saw Fiske and my neighbor, who had already testified on my behalf. Not one family member of mine was there; just strangers. I was brought to a chair and they uncuffed my hands from the belly chain. The judge asked me why I was crying so much, and if I had ever been in this much trouble. He asked me why I had committed this crime and what drove me to it.

Let me take a step back. After Fiske lost the extradition bus in West Virginia, he drove on to Maryland. From there, he arranged for his personal lawyer to be there at court to represent me.

The judge allowed me to be released on bail, with conditions, if I could come up with the money. Thanks to my father, who put up ten thousand dollars bail for me to be released, I was out. I was released with time served, and the judge decided he would enter me in pre-trial intervention, and the charges were dropped after the hearing. Even the bail money was returned to me, and receiving it helped to set up the apartment so I could see my son.

One of the conditions was that I be put in pre-trial intervention, as I said. I was told I could see my son after I secured an apartment, with all utilities, for six months, after which we would discuss the custody arrangement.

It felt as though it was finally over. I was free and I would see my son again, and the rest we would fight for once I was out. They took us back to our cells, where I waited to be released. It took longer than I expected. I was supposed to be released at 3 p.m. Well, that time came and went, and I must have fallen asleep, as the next thing I knew I heard the cell start to open. I heard the guard say my name and tell me to get my bed and bags. I was being released. I was so happy I jumped off the bed, missed the table to step on, and hit the floor. I had been on the top bunk and I landed hard. I broke my foot and leg. Lying on the floor in pain, my cellmate told me to not let them know I was hurt or they wouldn't release me; they would send me to the infirmary to heal before I could go.

She did not have to tell me twice! The guard came and asked if I was OK. I told them I was and began to walk in my chains with the bedroll and clothes in my arms, through long hallways and down the elevators, where Fiske was waiting for me to come out after being released. While being processed the guard must have seen the pain I was in, as he asked if I needed to see the doctor. I told him no, we continued with the release process, and I was sent to the gate area, where I was let out.

You have to know the picture I imagined after getting out was seeing my son and living happily ever after. Of course, that did not happen. What really happened was I had minutes to get out of the gated area before the gate closed. Fiske was yelling at me to run and I was hopping on one leg to freedom. I finally made it and fell on him as the gates from hell closed behind me. Once in the car I told Fiske what had happened to my leg.

The next day we had to go to court. I had to prepare for the custody hearing, clean up, and get some rest. He drove me to the rented motel room he had been staying in outside of Elkton, Maryland, just over the Delaware border outside of New Jersey. It was apparent he had been here the entire time I was in jail. He held mob meetings there to clear up his issues and get the hits off my family and me. He told me he also used the time to complete the deals he did not get to finish after getting caught up with me.

I walked into the motel room. He had a bath drawn and everything I needed to go to court in the morning to look presentable. *Only problem was my leg was now three times the normal size and purple. The pain was excruciating, to say the least.* But I dealt with it and made it through the first day of court. Afterward, at a deposition in my lawyer's office, the pain was so intense I had to leave to go to the emergency room. The X-rays showed I broke my foot on the right side and my shinbone was cracked. They set and cast my foot and leg, and I went back to court the next day. It was crazy between Harry and me at court that day. Amazingly, the threats were still flying, but Fiske kept him at bay.

It was now after Thanksgiving and I still had not been able to see my son. I had to wait until all leases and utility bills had been filed with the court and verified by the judge, and then wait for him to give the visitation order. His order was that I was allowed to see my son every Monday, Wednesday, and Friday. He would be with his father and his grandparents, who had moved into my home in New Jersey. Harry was hoping I would never get out, and they were planning to live there with Harry and help him raise my son.

Once all of the approvals were received in court that we had leased an apartment and had utilities paid for six months, we waited for the court to set up my first visitation with my son. Because I had no idea what had been told to my son, I wanted his coming to my apartment to feel like home. Fiske and I decided before the day came that we would drive all night to South Carolina so I could pick up some of his toys, clothes, and his race car bed. I wanted to have all of his things there when he arrived.

Once back to New Jersey we drove to the house to pick him up—and my heart broke. *His innocent face was gone and he did not know how to act when he saw me. He had been told I had left him and was not coming back.* He had been lied to about me and about everything that had happened. Once in the car I sat with him in the back and we held on to each other for a while. He told me he thought I did not love him anymore. I told him I had been in jail and if I could have been out sooner I would have come for him.

I was so angry with my husband for doing all of this to my son, a young child who had nothing to do with the situation between his father and me. All Harry had to do was be a grown-up and talk to him about what was happening to me and why he wasn't able to stay with either one of us. Instead he told him lies, cursed me in front of him, and hurt my child emotionally. Harry's pride, family name, and the fact that I had left him were his reasons for doing all of this to us. Not because he loved my son—no, revenge is what drove him.

~

The months that followed the divorce and custody hearings where horrible because Harry was in control, and it went to his head. He started to revert to his old self. He won custody. I had visitation privileges Monday, Wednesday, and Friday of each week. The rest of the week he would stay with Harry and his parents. But after some time Harry agreed that I could have him during the week and Harry would see our son on weekends. Then he was busy on the weekends, too.

Soon, I had my son all the time. During this time, my son was waging his own war. He did not want to be with his father and cried for hours during the time he was with Harry until we were together again. The weekly visitation pickup and the process of bringing him home were becoming violent. It was too much for my son and I to deal with.

Harry fell back into his old ways and, since the ordeal of me being on the run was over, Harry had no interest in visitation and would go for days without seeing or talking to our son.

As the six-month lease was running out, I wanted to come home to South Carolina. It was apparent Harry was not coming to see our son anymore, and I was bleeding money to pay for our lives in New Jersey and paying for our home and animals in South Carolina.

Months went by and, in April 1996, I called Harry and asked him what it would take for him to let us go home to South Carolina. After all, I was trapped in New Jersey for my "visitations." *My home was in South Carolina, and that was where I wanted to go: home.*

What Harry said he wanted was shocking, but showed his true colors. I had to sign over to him all of the rights to my home, the car I had bought and was not allowed to take, and all of the contents of the house, which included my clothes and the furniture I had before he even came into the picture. He only wanted the material stuff, and since I realized it was only, well, material things, it was worth letting it all go so we would be free and I would be able to take my son home to South Carolina.

After this conversation, I drew up the agreement with a carbon copy for Harry to keep. Fiske and I packed up the apartment where we had been living while my son was visiting his father on weekends.

We loaded the truck with all of our belongings and were at the door to my old home at 3 a.m. the next morning. Harry had signed the papers. I gave him his copy and was on my way home to South Carolina with my son.

It was all a done deal. I won, we were free, and we were on our way home together.

Fourteen

Death of My Parents

After we came home in April 1996, it seemed everything was behind us. My father was even there with my mother when we arrived. We were all so happy and relieved. All of our friends in the cul-de-sac came to greet us. Some of these people had come to my aid during the trial. I was finally home with my son, and we spent the days settling in to begin the rest of our lives.

A few days after arriving home in South Carolina, my father was having breathing issues and chest pains. He went into the hospital for three weeks. While in the hospital they performed what seemed like every test known to man. Yet they somehow missed the grapefruit-size aneurysm in his thoracic area. The hospital sent him home and told me he was a hypochondriac, that they had found nothing wrong with him.

I want to pause to say that during this entire ordeal my father stuck by my side. We became very close after I left home, talking on the phone daily. When my son and I came home he doted on and loved my son so much; this was the first grandchild he would be able to have a relationship with. His children, or his grandchildren from his other marriages, were not in contact with him, to my knowledge. During my entire life my father was very hard on me. But he was also always there with a card on every occasion; he never missed a holiday. He could love like no other; he was my best friend. Some may ask: how can someone who treated me horribly as a child be my best friend? I know now that his actions were what he believed was the proper way to discipline. *I also believe that the Lord placed forgiveness for my father on my heart.* My mother, on the other hand, was calm and caring, but she was not totally in her right mind. She was suspicious of everything I did. She became a bit elusive on where she was going and what she was doing.

My Father said he still felt the lump in his chest. I told him that he would have to just stop thinking about it, that they could not find anything. I drove him home, 18 hours away, and headed back to my home in South Carolina. *By the time I arrived at my home in the Carolinas, my father was rushed back to the hospital. He died in May 1996.*

It took me years to get over the death of my father. He was the only person I had in this world who was loyal and loved me like no other. He was my father, and now he was gone. We may have started out without the loving relationship a father and daughter should have, but we evolved into a relationship with love and respect. He stood by my side and believed in me through it all. He was so happy when it was all over, when my son and I could start a new life.

I drove him home and—unknowingly—left him there alone to die. Yes, he was a horrible person growing up, but he always showed me love and took care and protected me through everything and in every situation. When my father was planning his will several years earlier, he put my mother in charge of all the money and property. I begged him not to include my son's money and mine in his will as my mother would never let us have it. He could not believe my mother would hurt me, so he did not take my warning. God had to help me get my joy back after his death; I simply was not able to do it on my own.

I have to say I loved my mother and we were very close when I was young. When I worked at the hospital with her we would go to the doctors' and holiday parties together. We really became close before I was married to my first husband in 1982. But as a grown-up, she and I differed in many areas.

While I was on the run I would pawn and pay off the jewelry that I had received over the years; these choices paid the rent, utilities, and groceries. My mother was not happy about me using my jewelry. I knew I would get it back eventually, but this is not what tore apart our relationship. What happened was my mother loved her jewels and valued them, so she never sold or pawned anything she had. To her, no reason in the world could ever warrant such an action. To me, my son having a roof over his head, meals, and clothes on his back—these things were more important than jewelry. Over the 18 months on the run, I had pawned lots of jewelry to keep us afloat. When I had to drive back and forth to New Jersey every other weekend, it became very expensive, and difficult, to make the payments, and yet somehow I did. My mother thought Fiske should take care of us, But we were not a couple and I would not be in debt to him either. I was going to be free from owing anybody a favor for giving me money for my family.

While we were in New Jersey, my mother never paid the pawn tickets, and I lost all of the jewelry that I had had since I was a child. Some of the pieces I loved were from all the years my parents bought me birthday gifts and family pieces that were purchased for me as a child. These were rare items I never would have again. Although I loved having and wearing the jewelry, it was worth more to have my son and meet his needs.

My mother continued to live with me after we returned to South Carolina, but we had a very strained relationship. She took care of my son but did nothing to help me. My mother heard my father was sick and might die; she left South Carolina and went to New York. While my father was in the hospital she cleaned out all of the bank accounts and closed them all. She sent all the money, every penny, including my father's money for my son and I, off to her son from a previous marriage. She gave him the right to handle getting it to my son and I; he became the executor of my parents' estates. He had not seen or talked to my parents or me in 30 years.

It was October 1996, and I had no idea she had done this. One night in November of the same year, she never came home. Some might not have worried and said, "Who cares?" But I still loved her and she was my mother. No matter how rotten she had been to me, I still loved her and did not want anything to happen to her. I called every hospital and morgue until I found her in the same hospital in which my father had died.

She had terminal lung and ovarian cancer and had had a stroke from an overdose of chemotherapy and radiation; she was comatose. As soon as I found her and heard about her condition, I ran to the hospital to find her. After I had been visiting for a while on one of my visits the phone rang; it was her son. After calling me names, he was happy to tell me that I was not getting a dime of mine and my son's inheritance, that he had it all.

I was so angry that I told my comatose mother that I didn't care what she did to me, but to leave us penniless was so wrong. I was just trying to grasp it all. When she woke up, she said she was so sorry she did it, and she asked how we could get it back. I was shocked at her waking up after seven weeks; had she been in a coma all the time, or just when I was there? I learned that she had signed her health care rights and decisions over to her son's care. She sent him all of our money: thousands of dollars of jewelry estate pieces from her mother from Italy, and the deeds to her land in Florida and my father's home where I grew up in New York.

My mother's son's plan was to stick her in a home until she died. I told him: you can have the money, but I have my mother. She may "hate me," but she had lived with me for the past 20 years! I was not going to let that happen to her. I may have been upset with her about the will, but I couldn't let this man put her in a home to be forgotten about like her family had done to *her* mother. *I made that promise to her at 16 because of what happened to my grandmother.*

My grandmother was very wealthy when she began to lose her mind and wander. My mother's brother decided to put her in a home under an assumed name. He had a lawyer redo all of her documents to reflect he was caring for her and her affairs, he named himself executor, and he made the entire inheritance his. None of my mother's siblings received anything that was promised in the original will. No one knew what he was doing. We always checked on my grandmother; one day we went to see her and she was gone. After calling all around town and the family, my mother finally talked to her brother, and he told her he put my grandmother in a home. Of course, there was an argument and we started to search for her, but we did not know the name he had her listed under. We did not find her until she was about to die, and he called us all to allow us to say our good-byes. I never wanted to see her suffer. She was my grandmother. It was at this point that I told my mother I would never let that happen to her. My mother quickly answered me: "I will never need you to care for me." Wow, was she wrong.

After the shock of hearing all this had worn off, I went into care mode and was at the hospital every day, cleaning, caring for her, making sure she was getting the help she needed. It took me a month to get all the paperwork overturned so that my mother could come home and live with me until she died. She had to be psychiatrically evaluated. This would determine if this was what she wanted to do, and without being coerced. *So the health care power of attorney was overturned and her care given to me. I took my mother home with me to care for her until her death.*

People thought I was crazy to take her into my home and care for her after all my mother had done to me through the years. Some told me I should let her go to a home. But I knew I could not sleep at night not knowing if she was being properly cared for. She was given six months to live; hospice was called in as she was fully loaded with cancer. I had to try to give her a chance to live as long as she could, so I started her on the Gherson Diet, which is a holistic treatment to fight cancer. It was a detox cancer program where we juiced all kinds of fruit and vegetables to rid her of the diseases. She had to drink one every hour on the hour! I would mix up the different items and give one to her every day, 24 hours a day, for 6 months. She had difficulty swallowing food and water, so they put a tube in her stomach, and this made it so much easier to get all the drinks, food and medication I had to grind up to feed her with little fuss.

Well, she did not pass in the six months. She became stronger and even walked again! I took her everywhere she wanted to go, and she ate all of the food she craved and wanted to eat. We became close at her end all was for-given. But she too passed away in May, two days after the anniversary date of my father's death in 1998. During the time my mother was dying, I sold the mobile home we were living in. We needed more room for her care.

By this time I had started up a military surplus and supply company in the local flea market and had six booths full of merchandise. I made great money on the weekends, enough to support the family every month. After my father died, Fiske stayed to help me with the land and set-up of the homes, as I had too much on my plate.

I found a 10-acre tract in Bonneau Beach. We broke ground, installed the septic and water lines, cleared the trees, and put a modular home on the back. We cleared six acres and then another acre in front. I loved the land and homes and began to put the infrastructure in as we went along.

I had come into some money; this helped me take these steps and pay off my mother's debt and her funeral expenses. We lived here after we moved out of the trailer we had lived in while on the run, and I thought we would be in our new home for a while. Anyone who knows me knows I love ani-mals. We rescued two dogs, then three more that needed help. One had puppies, so that made more mouths to feed. Then came a pot-bellied pig name Delilah, and after her came another pig, until we had six little pig-gies and several dogs. By the time my mother passed we had twelve dogs, many pot-bellied pigs, and a pink pig that belonged to an elderly neighbor who had passed away. He left me his large, hateful pig, named Petunia. People were trying to leave animals at the front of my driveway. They knew I would not abandon them, that they would be taken care of.

Every day was a feat in itself to get through. My son was in school, my mother was dying . . . and yes, Fiske the satanic contractor was becoming more and more evil and destructive. He loved fires, so Fiske would get burn permits and set the woods on fire while he was drinking the night away. Some of the fires became deadly. Then it was all hands and feet on deck, as we had to get out the hoses and stomp out the fires before they burned our houses down. He would drink for hours and come in around 3 a.m. His eyes were always black and I knew he needed to be watched. After drinking all day I had to feed him a full meal so he would not get delusional and attempt to shoot everyone. He was out of control, and a few times I had to jump his back to get the weapons out of his hands. He would be drunk and laughing, but I wasn't afraid of him and would jump on his back to stop him. He said he got a charge out of me being feisty. Feisty I was, stopping him from shooting my son, me my mother, or the neighbors.

It was brutal living with him. He was shooting my mother's drugs into his body and drinking. It was the same drama every night: drink the night away with friends and come inside to eat and go to sleep. I made sure the food was ready so he would nod off and I could finally go to sleep.

I had a dream that Fiske had shot my son, and I knew this was God warning me. With the care of my mother and raising my son, along with the antics of the evil one, all the animals, and six flea market booths—it all became too much for me. After my mother passed away, I began to think of ways out.

In September 1999 I found out I had cancer, and this changed everything.

I know this story is full of destruction and despair. But *God gave me the strength to work my way through it all. I look back now and wonder how I did it.* Thanks be to God, as He never gives us more than we can handle.

Fifteen

Beating Cancer and Starting Over . . . Again

Finding out I had cervical cancer was like being hit with a sledgehammer. I had had health issues since the age of 15. But now I began to panic; how could this be happening to me? The only two people I ever had in my life were my parents. My family members treated me like a leper. No calls, no help, just snide remarks and comments. One cousin came down to see my mother before she passed, and that was the last time I saw any other family member or had any family help.

I was alone and Fiske was off the deep end drinking and doing so many drugs; I could not even keep track of them. Although I had not given my life to Jesus yet, I was still praying to my invisible God, hoping He would have mercy and let me live. *I started to pray and ask God to save me so I could raise my son right.* I did not want him to go back to his father, and I did not have any friends or family to take care of my son if I died. At this point in our relationship, Fiske and I hated each other, and he was hoping I would leave.

I begged and pleaded with God: if he let me live I would change and be what he wanted me to be. Well, that fateful day came. In November 1999 I was admitted for cancer surgery. For five days I had to leave my precious child alone with the most evil man I had ever known. I could not trust his father to care for him and thus give him back to me when I came out of the hospital. All the people I could trust with my son were gone. Even though my parents were violent and my mother's true colors had come out during the trial, I knew if anything happened to me she would care for my son. But Harry was not an option.

I went through the surgery and for five days worried about my son. I asked God to protect him because I was unable to be there. To this day I do not know what happened to him while in the care of this evil person. My son didn't talk about it then and still hasn't today. I have tried to get him to tell me about those days. He will not talk about it.

During my stay in the hospital I was so drugged up I did not know who came in and who did not. When I did wake up, I asked if I had any calls or visitors and was told no one had called or come to visit. I wondered where my son and Fiske were; he did not answer the phone, and we did not have cell phones at that time. Finally it came time for me to leave the hospital. I was discharged in the morning. I waited all day and no one came for me. By 5 p.m. I was waiting on the steps of the hospital with my suitcase, in my pajamas, waiting for Fiske to pick me up. It was cold and Fiske didn't show up until much later in the evening. I was in so much pain when I arrived home that I was taken back to the hospital by ambulance because Fiske refused to take me. The next day I came home by cab since Fiske was no-where to be found. Sick and in pain, my son took care of me until I could get up and walk around. This child had been through more in his nine years than many people have by the time they are in their sixties.

After a horrible dream that showed my son being killed, I knew it was an-other of my warning dreams, and I started to plan an escape. Every day while everyone was away, I walked my figure-eight 650-foot driveway from my rental home in the front of my land to the back part of the land where my home was. I did this until I could walk straight up and strong since I had been so weak from surgery.

The last straw came, and I realized I had to choose the way I wanted to live my life. I had lived surrounded by evil for seven years and had been pushed to accept Fiske's satanic beliefs. And then I saw something so frightening I made my decision in one heartbeat. One night after Fiske was on a drink-ing binge from morning until 3 a.m., I turned to look at him and what I saw in his eyes freaked me out. *It was at that moment I made the decision to walk with God and that I wanted no part of the dark side I had been dabbling with my entire life.* This was serious; as the fear hit my heart I knew I had to go. When I looked in his eyes I saw black circles and flames in his corneas and pupils. This was confirmation that he was as evil as his actions had become after my parents had passed. My son and I were in danger. God was giving me warning dreams to change my course in life or we would pay dearly.

The hunt began to get out and turn to the God I had always talked to when I needed him to bail me out.

I started seeing advertisements in the paper for a room for rental, ocean-front rooms for $95 a week on Folly Beach. I knew I needed to get there and check it out. I had to leave Fiske and the time was now; we had to go. I told no one about the plan. I knew I needed a place to jump to regroup and heal. So I found a home in my neighborhood as I had asked Fiske to leave and he would not. He stole $11,000 from me and told me he was robbed. Everyone who knew him feared him; who would dare come up against him? We moved into this dumpy trailer and I had a chance to heal and plot a plan. After moving into the trailer around the corner from my house, a doctor's post-op visit found I had broken loose the stitches from surgery after moving. So I was faced with having repair surgery to fix the incision from a previous hysterectomy.

We were safe at last—or were we? We came home one night and something was not right. My dog was scared and there were footprints throughout the house. At first we thought it was our landlord, but I called him, and he had not come by. It was my super sleuth son who found a tiny ash on the floor and we knew it was Fiske. He came to see if we had food and the prints showed his steps.

After this I knew we needed to run, to move again. I went to a Christmas party at this place in Folly Beach where I had seen the ad about the rooms for rent. On the way I was in dreamland; I pictured a nice big rooming house. When we arrived, what a place it was. I said to the Lord, "Great. I'm leaving hell and going to Sodom and Gomorrah." But still, at least the room we had was clean and had its own bathroom. I was now working as a terminal manager for a national trucking company, and I was making great money, an income that would care for us.

A young man I knew for a few years while at my land, came to me after being kicked out of his home by his mother and ran to me for help. He and his girlfriend were living with us at the time I fled from Fiske. He was afraid of Fiske and did not want to stay with out me there, he saw too much too.

The manager of the Front Beach Inn put the teenagers that came with me, in a room downstairs and we had a room next to the manager's room, upstairs, for safety; the manager's floor was always peaceful. I started to love this place even though most of the tenants here had issues with drugs and alcohol. I cannot judge anyone, as I don't want to be judged. Plus, living in such close quarters, they all knew how I was with my son, and that I would not tolerate anyone doing anything to him. *I had shown the mother wolf side a few times, and all began to naturally look out for us.* Once settled, I became friends with the other tenants, as most were good people who just had their issues. Most had respect for me and took a liking to my son. I was a mom first and foremost. I didn't go to the bars or hang out; I worked and went home. Living in this apartment was great; there were no huge responsibilities, just the weekly rent (we had all utilities included). My son was safe, I had a good job, we were on the ocean, and we had the beach as our playground. After we settled in, the other people in the rooming house started to look out for us.

But my son was a very sick child, and the doctors could not figure out why he was so ill. He was homeschooled at the rooming house for his entire fifth grade year. Because he was sick he had to stay home during the day, and two teenagers watched him while I was at work.

Everything was going great at my job, until one day my boss never showed up at the office. I called his friend and asked him to go check to see if he was home. It turned out he had had a heart attack and died, and now the business and office were up for sale. After my boss died, we became a million-dollar team for two years in sales. Our company did better after he was gone than when he was alive.

After a couple of years on our own running the office and keeping it all going without our boss, another man bought the company. We thought the new owner would love walking into a thriving business and not having to rebuild it, but all he wanted it for was a tax write-off. He fired me and the main dispatcher and killed the company.

All during the years after my son was born, I had to work in severe pain due to an accident in 1984. This made me unable to keep a nine-to-five job. My body just gave out trying to heal from cancer surgery, so I took a job on the beach in the town's grocery store. This was great; I lived across the street and was home for my son.

We eventually moved into the apartment above the store with a new friend I met at the rooming house who had driven up from Florida for work. Moose—this is what we will call my roommate for this story—was a good guy and we became great friends and roommates when we decided to chip in to share the rent and utilities. With my son being home alone and my work hours long, I decided a roommate would be great to have, someone who could be there for him when I worked late. We became great friends; my son had the master bedroom and Moose had the second bedroom. I slept in my recliner in the living room as I wanted my son to have his space, and Moose was paying to live in the apartment; it was only right he have his own space too. I didn't mind; we had a great place in the heart of the beach with an ocean view and all the action from tourists bustling around town. And I did not have to go out to see what was going on as everyone came to the grocery store; this store is a landmark in Folly Beach.

Because I only knew Moose for a few months, I would monitor everything he did. I didn't want bar-hoppers coming home with him, and since my son and I had just come out of a horrible situation, I was not going to have it all over again here. Moose turned out to be a great roommate, even though he was working through his own issues. We remained roommates until he bought his own house and moved out eight years later.

It was in the apartment over the grocery store that my son started becoming ill with sinus infections that would form a tough, leather-like seal covering his sinus cavities. He would have to have surgery to open them up, and this condition lasted until 2013. Moose's family was awesome, and his mother, Annie, even came up from Florida to care for my son during the time he had to have sinus surgery and needed someone to be there to help him recuperate when Moose and I had to work. Moose and I are friends to this day and he is happily married. My son had terrible headaches and the neurologists could not figure out what was causing them. He would have such horrible pain that he would have some type of seizure, his eyes would roll back into his sockets, and his lips would turn blue. I would have to massage his neck for him to have relief. The doctors had to give him painkillers to endure the pain. But I knew that God had brought us here to Folly, as one of my customers at the store was a local man who was a chiropractor.

One day during my store shift this man came in and asked how we were doing. I opened up to him and explained what was going on. God had sent a chiropractor who specialized in what was wrong with my son; it turned out to be the atlas in his neck. The atlas is the bone in the upper part of the spine that connects your skull to your spine. The atlas holds the skull securely in place. My son's was out of place and, being out of place, it had the nerves in his neck twisted out of place. After the first visit all of his symptoms started to dissipate and they began to disappear with continued treatments. God softened the heart of this kind chiropractor as he agreed to work with me for the payments and even began to treat us both. Praise

God for divine intervention!

When my son was 5, after a freak accident while playing, which led to him being taken to the emergency room, they performed a CAT-scan of his head and found he had a subarachnoid cyst in his head. A subarachnoid cyst is a fluid-filled sac of spinal fluid that forms a sac in the middle of the brain. It is like an aneurysm, but more stable; he was born with it and it took up space in the lower part of his brain. This cyst needed monitoring for the next eight years, until he was 15. He still has it today, but God has kept it all together for him to live a normal life.

God really opened the hearts of so many strangers to accept us and nurture us back to life. As strangers treated us with love and kindness, it restored my faith in people considering all those I had dealt with in life up to that point.

All was well for quite a while, and I began to love Folly Beach and called the island home. We were accepted and taken under the wings of the locals who lived here. But even in paradise my world seemed to find a way to fall apart. It seemed drugs, booze, or both always intoxicated nearly everyone in the store I worked in. They would call in sick because they knew I lived upstairs and would come down and pick up hours. Finally, the owners hired a popular person in the community to be the new store manager.

We were evicted on a weeks' notice two weeks later; we were homeless again. The new manager took over and everything was changed. While my son was recovering from sinus surgery, we were given the eviction notice; my son was terrified that we would be thrown out on the street. I did go have a few choice words with this new manager about serving a 9 year old.

An older woman I worked with told me we could live at her house on a nearby island. She also offered to let me buy it if I agreed to do the repairs. I would not have to pay rent or make any payments until it was done. Being so trusting, little did I know the house was already in foreclosure. We did all the repairs to the floors, doors, and plumbing, and all new appliances were put in. There were a lot of bugs in this place, but it had potential and it was going to be mine, so I knew I had to do it right. Weeks went by and it was getting colder and we did not have central heat. I slept in the living room, which had a belly stove. I would load it with wood all night long to keep the fire going. We had a fan; I used it to blow the heat into my son's room.

One night I was in so much pain with my back I could not move. I had to throw shoes that were near me at the wall next to Moose's bedroom to call for help. With Moose's help, I was finally able to get to the recliner.

I wanted so much to relax and just deal with all of the pain. Then I heard in my mind: *Change the channel on the TV.* I wasn't sure who was telling me to change the channel, but I did it, and then I heard *STOP! When I had stopped changing channels, an evangelical preacher named JM was on TV talking about God. I was like, OK, now what? Am I going nuts hearing voices in my head? And now religion is the answer? Yeah, OK.* Then I heard: *Shut up and listen.* JM started wagging her finger at the television, saying, "Someone out in TV land needs to hear this. God has a plan for your life." Even though I was not saved, even broken and sick, it would all turn around, JM said. I started to laugh and didn't want to believe she was talking about me. She was a lot like me, truthfully—kind of harsh, but she kept going and I kept listening and listening. To this day JM has been my link to learning all about God, and her books have changed my life.

Several months later I was told I could buy the little island house. But while waiting for HUD to approve my loan, I found out about it being in foreclosure for months, and that it had been auctioned off. All that work I had put into it to make it livable for someone else!

After having nowhere to live once again, I reached out to an older lady who became like a grandmother to me and my son. Her name was Miss Emily; we were working together and were quite the team in the grocery store on Folly. She has been a local since the Sixties and knew everyone on the beach, so she reached out to the landlord of one of the homes she managed. It was a sweet little two-bedroom bungalow across the street and around the corner from the grocery store. We moved in and Moose was still with us at this time, so once again the bedrooms were taken and I was still in my recliner in the living room. All was great here. We were back on Folly and I was home. Now I just had to find a new job.

My son started sixth grade at his new school. This is where he met his mentor and English teacher, Chuck Long, who had taken an interest in my son and saw his musical and acting talents. Chuck began asking my son to read out loud in class, and my son was really getting attached to this teacher. Chuck was the only positive male role model he had up to this point in life, as well as someone who took an interest in him. At the end of sixth grade Chuck asked if my son would try out for the Charleston Youth Company (CYC), a theater company for talented children. Applying students had to keep up their grades and work hard to be part of the company. My son ended up performing with this company at the Sotille Theatre in Charleston, South Carolina until he graduated from high school. Chuck and his family became my son's family. He fit well with the theater company and went on to make lifelong friends. I loved being involved with all of the show's backstage helping to create the costumes was my way of helping out. It was this family that I requested to care for my son if anything happened to me. The entire family loved my son so much they agreed. Thank God they said yes, as I could not have asked for a better family to love my son than Chuck and his family.

So my son chose music education and theater arts as his career path. His years performing with CYC gave him the performance bug. God gave my son the ability to play music by ear, and He also gave him the ability to pick up any instrument he was given the opportunity to try.

In 2008 my son graduated from high school. He had been asked to sing the national anthem for the opening ceremony. I have always been extremely proud of all my son has overcome in his life. Every show I went to while he was performing with CYC, I cried. I was in awe of his talent and how amazing his voice was during musical performances. When he began to sing there were the usual hecklers, but as he sang before an audience of hundreds who had filled the North Charleston Colisseum for the graduation ceremony, they began to cheer and clap at his version of the anthem. He received a standing ovation and could not erase his smile for hours. I was, of course, in tears and beaming with love and amazement at what my boy was becoming with the help of the Lord.

My son is my greatest accomplishment. God taught me how to love and break the cycle of violence so my son could have the life I always dreamed and prayed for him to have. He went on to attend a Christian college, in Newberry South Carolina, studying music education. I guess the music I would play with headphones on my stomach helped him before he was born; it helped make him who he is today. He loves all kinds of music genres, as I do.

God has brought us through a journey to where the prayers of a lost mother—offerings prayed years ago for my son's destiny—have been answered. We were where we were meant to be for him to begin his life in God's world. As a child I kept my son in children's church and Bible study so he could learn more of God, and all this has kept him on the path to his destiny.

By the way, neither of us had a clue this was happening until we were saved years later, and he was in college.

My son has become the young adult I hoped he would be. Strong, loved, and he has had so many friends and opportunities come to him. I wanted his life to be stable once we made it out and started over, so I tried not to move him away from Folly Beach. This way he would belong and have the lifelong friends. This is always what I longed for but did not have until I met my BFF Roseanne in high school.

My son had a good life here until he moved away from home to pursue his dreams in the theater industry. Praise Jesus for answering my prayers for his life.

Sixteen

A New Opportunity, a Fresh Start

After years of being told I would never accomplish anything in life, having this new job gave me hope things were finally starting to turn around. This accomplishment was my first step to knowing I was on the road to the recovery of our finances, and that my son and I would be OK. I felt as long as I could work, everything would be fine, and we would make it through. I told myself: *I can take care of us. I'm a self-sufficient person, right?*

That's what I thought. I had the mind-set that I didn't need anything or anyone. *But it wasn't long before I learned how invaluable depending on the Lord, rather than myself, was.* God showed me it wasn't my own doing that got us back on the right track—it was Him. He is a loving Father who provides for us every day.

Shortly after moving back to Folly, I was on the hunt for a job that would give us security. I found a listing in the paper for a vacation rental company as a reservations clerk. I could not support my son and I on seven dollars an hour, which is what the grocery store paid. I went for the interview knowing I did not have any experience in the real estate vacation rental/hospitality industry. The interview went great and I was hired on the spot. I was both shocked and nervous because I did not have dress clothes! I was so poor I did not have anything I could wear to work. But for some reason, they took a liking to me and put up with my attire until I could buy more professional clothes. I made them laugh and showed leadership abilities and after several months I realized I was being thrown into every aspect of the vacation rental business. This entailed helping families from all over the world book the right home for their vacations. I also booked homes that were specifically dedicated for oceanfront weddings. We were concierges and were on call 24 hours a day in case our guests needed anything.

It was a great fit for me because I love to talk to people and make sure all their needs are met. After about a year the property manager had a falling out with the bookkeeper. I was promoted to property manager after she quit. I had to pass the real estate test for the license I would need for this position. I studied night and day, thinking, *I am too old to do this; I hate tests!* After two months of falling asleep with the books on my lap the day came for the test. I arrived at the test site two hours early and studied some more. I walked into the testing area with six others and we sat down and began the two-hour test.

I was so nervous and the questions seemed too easy; I was waiting for the hard questions. So many people have failed this test and had to take it several times. I was not the sharpest tool in the shed after all that had gone on in my life. I did not think I would stand a chance, but I went for it anyway. The pressure was on me to pass this test, as I did not want to blow the opportunity for my son and I as well as those in the real estate company who were giving me the chance to change our lives for the better. As I answered the questions I soon realized I had come to the exam's end and I had only been in the room about 20 minutes. I became scared as I thought I might have done something wrong to the computer. All kinds of thoughts were going through my mind. I finally mustered the courage to go to the examiner overseeing the tests.

As I walked past the others still in the midst of taking the two-hour test, I was afraid I had not finished and would not be able to complete the exam. I walked out of the testing room into the waiting area, but no one was in the outer room. I waited.

A man walked back into the room and was surprised to see me standing there. I told him I thought I broke the computer and did not know what to do. So he went over to his computer which was hooked to all of our testing terminals and looked at my test. He started to laugh. I was so nervous, as my life and future, I was sure, depended on this test—and this man was laughing! I asked him, "What's so funny?" He told me I had not broken the computer but had completed the test; we were both shocked! Then I asked him if I passed. He said he could not tell me, but that he was going to get some water and I could possibly peek at the computer screen and my score. It was like a conspiracy movie; I had to wait till he left the room, and then, slowly, I meandered over to his computer to look at my score. Then I saw it. I didn't believe it, and would never have guessed at this. I was hoping to pass, but instead God gave me a 100 percent in only 20 minutes of taking this test! I left that building screaming and hollering, "Thank you, Jesus!"

I was not even saved yet, so this for me was amazing as I thought my brain could not learn new things after all I had been through. *Our amazing Lord can do anything he wants to us and in us.* I went back to the office, where they already knew my score. I was now the new property manager of this real estate company on the beach. *It's amazing how God can take us from rags to riches in a hot New York second.* Only at the time, I did not know it was him. I thought it was me, and I was amazed at myself that I could have accomplished this.

During my time at the real estate company we flourished with the addition of more long-term and vacation rentals. With the sales side of the company picking up, we became competitive with the other real estate companies on the beach. I hired three more people to carry all the many vacation rental bookings from all the homes I had added to our company's roster of oceanfront homes.

After I had worked at the real estate company on the beach for two years, I heard we were having financial issues. I wondered why: we had many homes and the maintenance and other costs were low.

Due to the sensitive nature of this issue, all I'm going to say is that I found errors and told the owner of the company.

Well, guess who was fired? Me of course. I found out I was let go as I was coming to bring a doctor's note in for a sprained ankle to cover my absence that day. As I arrived at the office the locks were being changed. This broke my heart, as I truly loved this job, and the homeowners—well, their homes were like my own. I would be out sandbagging the office and homes by myself when storms would come to prevent flooding on the oceanfront and across-the-street homes. I was on call 24/7 for anyone who needed help. I loved going to work when I was with this company. *My departure from the company was very sad; I went into seclusion for months. I would cry and ask God, Why?* Then came the calls from owners of the houses I managed, plus a lot of people from town were calling me to tell me to keep my head up and that they didn't believe the rumors. But I simply could not get a job anywhere on the beach after this. I found out years later what the reason was that had been told to everyone; to say I was heartbroken because I trusted some of those who worked with me that I hired and thought were my friends—this would be an understatement. This was one of my favorite jobs. We had floats in the holiday parades; our company was active in the community events throughout the year. But it was the owners' appreciation of our hard work and the love of the beautiful oceanfront homes we were taking care of that I loved the most.

There is a comical point to this story. Another of God's leadings told me to go to my office as they were changing the locks. The best part of this whole story shows God at work. Because we went straight home after my appointment and were parked in the driveway when I suddenly had the urging to go back to the office. I did not go to the office to drop off the note at first; my son came with me to the doctor's office and I heard in my spirit to go give the note *now*. I told my son to come with me to turn in the note. He wasn't happy and said, "Mom we're home. I just want to go in." I told him it would only take a minute—and then he saw it all unfold as evil showed its ugly head again.

Seventeen

My Journey with God and Hearing from Him

During my time at the real estate company, a Realtor friend I worked with told me he had a client with a nice condominium with three bedrooms and three baths on the marsh. It had enough room for Moose, my son, and me to all live comfortably. The bonus was I would have a bedroom; finally a real bedroom all to myself. And I would have my own bath for the first time in ten years. Remember, I had been sleeping in a recliner in the living room so my son and Moose could each have a bedroom and since my mother was sick to be closer to her room so I could hear her if she needed me. With this place we could live and finally have a home, I could finally rest quietly, and I could have a door to close out the world. God knew it was time for me to have a room of my own to be still and hear his voice.

I had the keys to take a look at the condo, but a hurricane was beginning to really blow, and I decided to see if it was safe in high winds, because the bungalow we were in at the time was scary during hurricanes. I love a good storm and was out riding around checking the beach homes for damage or lines down, and I decided to go check it out. I immediately fell in love with it. I love to sit and look at the marsh view that stretches out for miles. *The ocean and river tides would fill the marsh at high tide, and the wildlife made me feel as if I had my own private sanctuary while I was living on the ocean. God is good to me,* as that was a dream I had had since being a child. I took the condo and we moved in to the only real home my son and I ever had that lacked drama. We were finally safe and comfortable. For me, having a bedroom for the first time in ten years was like a rebirth. I had a deck and privacy to just think and gather calming thoughts. *It would be here I would come face to face with the One who had been providing for and guiding me during the past years of our lives.*

Folly Beach has always been a God experience for me. I was not here for the parties or people, I was here because God led me here. I was not interested in a social life; I needed time to reflect on what we had overcome, and simply to rest. I became a homebody as my room became my safe haven to relax and think and be with my son and enjoy the amenities that came with the condo. Our second- floor condo faced the pool, and my son and his friends enjoyed having a huge pool to call home when the beach was inundated with tourists. The visitors would grow our tiny community of 1,600 year-round locals to more than ten thousand during the summer months. Moose was a great friend, and we struggled to survive together through all of each other's job changes and life challenges. After several years with Moose as a roommate, he found a great state job and moved out when he purchased his own home.

After the loss of my job at the real estate company, my son going off to college, and Moose moving out, I was alone and on my own for the first time in decades. I was becoming weaker and my body was hurting all the time. I had no idea what was wrong with me, and I simply wasn't ready to go to the doctor and hear any bad news.

I had fought depression since I was 5 because of all the betrayal in my life. My friends, family, my mother, and the men I married had all betrayed me and my son when we were in dire need of their help and support. *The only one I could ever count on was my dad, and he was gone.* I have suffered from depression since being a very young child. Now was no different than before; my spirit was beaten and feeling ready to give up. Though the Scriptures say that God will not give us more than we can handle, I was wondering where my end would be. People who knew me would never think I was sick. But I stopped going out unless I had to go for the mail or walk the dogs. My son was in college and I was living alone with my dogs, but they both suddenly passed away too. It seemed everyone I loved was leaving me or dying off.

Whenever life became overwhelming before I knew the Lord I would panic, worry, and pace the house trying to figure a way out. *I did not know that I only had to give up my pride and ego and reach out for God's hand.*

I just wanted out of this roller coaster hell that I called my life. As a child, suicide was always on my mind; it was a possible way out. I didn't like life or myself. Life was just too hard. I was tired of the struggle and the fight to survive.

But because of this angelic boy God had placed in my life, this child who truly loved me, I determined to get him on his feet first before I could check out. After all, once he was on his feet and grown, he would leave me too. So at least he would be set if I left an insurance policy with some cash in it so he could take care of himself. *I was not thinking straight, and it showed. I was full of anger, bitterness, and feeling betrayed and alone.* All I wanted to do was run away. That is what I always did, and I felt it was what I needed to do: run away from pain inflicted on me by others. After all, I had left three homes I bought, and all of my furniture and clothes that were in the homes I also left behind, all to avoid more pain. So why would now be any different?

I started to hear much more from the Lord as I went walking on the beach at night, and I was still healing and recovering from my past. I had to learn to forgive and walk away from all of the horrible memories and leave my past behind forever. I had to overcome and go on to a new life with the Lord. *Which is not easy, as it means we have to change the default patterns we run to when our emotions are running wild.*

Gone were all the remarks from all of the voices of my past. We all hear from the people in our lives. Plus, from the evil one, who works to always keep us in the doom and gloom of our lives to make sure we stay in a "condemned state" from our mistakes. I have learned that is *not* what God thinks about us; we just need to feel his love and have faith in him. This was a daily battle for me since my mind was all over the place with doubt. Doubt in myself to be able to keep going. We have to choose good thoughts to get past the memories of our past.

One morning as I watched JM preaching, she talked about the battlefield of the mind and how to grasp control over one's thoughts. She helped me see I had to renew my mind each day with what the Word of the Lord says about us and who we are in Him. Once we ask Him to forgive us, and we move forward with Him, He will bring us into alignment with what He has planned for our lives. But I did not know his words yet. I was still struggling with my inner issues. My grief, bitterness, and anger took over my mind and I could not see a way out. I know I was changing, but I was still in between who I was and who I wanted to be. Confusion and illnesses would once again begin to take over.

I'm not saying it was easy. On the contrary, I am telling you it was very hard, and I was not dedicated to Jesus and could not see the love God had for me—yet. But the seed of love was in my heart. I had locked it off from being hurt so many times. Although I thought I was alone throughout most of my life—from my youth to becoming an adult—I wasn't. *Every time I felt overwhelming fear, Jesus was always there; I just did not know Him or think He knew me.* It seems funny now, but at the time when I thought I was talking to myself about my issues, I was really talking to Jesus. I just didn't know it! No one understood me better than myself—so I thought. Until one day when this soft voice inside me started answering me on issues that had plagued my mind as a child. Who were my parents, really? Because after their deaths I uncovered stuff I had never heard of. He led me to those who had answers, and to websites to gather information I needed to use to solve the puzzle I called my life.

I hoped with all my heart that my life had some kind of purpose, or I would not have survived all I had been through. I was scared at first. I thought I was losing my mind from being on my own after all of the stress I had lived with since childhood. This voice was not audible; I felt it in my spirit. It was a calming, loving voice that was discussing times in my life no one else knew about—no one but my parents and I. The events in my life were now being explained to me. I had to start to have an open heart. I have heard this voice all throughout my life, but I thought it was *my* decisions or thoughts coming to their own conclusions.

By the time I asked God to forgive me and teach me his way, I was totally distrustful of religion. I thought that if I was going to dedicate my life to Him and believe in what I could not see and touch, I needed to *hear it* from Him. I didn't trust the church or its people, as all through my life "church" represented fear, judgment, and that I would always be a sinner. Churches don't talk about having a relationship with Jesus, his grace, or the forgiveness of a loving Father as our God. To me, church was all about the priest's agenda or some theology. The Catholic Church doesn't teach the Bible to us; it has its own set of doctrine it teaches. *Condemnation and penance was the normal way of life. I always wondered why would anyone want to live this way.* I always took God for a loving, forgiving person from what I saw from the preachers on TV and the Easter and Christmas shows I grew up watching as a child. Three of my favorite Easter shows that affected me as a child, into adult life, were the original *King of Kings*, *The Robe*, and *Jesus of Nazareth*. I waited for those shows to come on every year, because that is what I felt, even as a child, our loving God was like. What I find remarkable about myself is I have always been a dreamer and so hopeful about what my future holds. Throughout my entire life I always believed in a better tomorrow. *That this invisible God was really there and knew who I was, but that because of my sins he wasn't going to help me until I became a good person. And this was so far from the truth.*

I always loved my parents and, although life with them was hard, it does not matter what they did to me. I know they loved my son and me, and forgiveness has healed my heart. My father and I were very close when I was a child; we would play cards and board games. Even though his discipline was harsh, it was the only love I knew. He took me everywhere with him on the motorcycle. And at the end of his life we made amends. He always stuck by my side through everything that was going on. My mother and I were close during my childhood and teen years; she was always trying to protect me from the brutal beatings I would get for sticking up for her when she was getting hit. My father, being a strong-minded and stubborn man, didn't see me as a child protecting her mother. My father thought I was taking her side and ganging up on him, even though he was out of control.

My mother was the ultimate shopaholic, as I shared earlier, while I was growing up, and she was always buying me expensive clothes, coats, and jewelry. The same jewelry she left at the pawn shop and didn't make payments on. She had her own stash of money that she kept hidden and thought my father didn't know about. But my father knew everything she did; he just never said anything to her. He would see me in new clothes, and we never lacked for anything. Christmases were huge in our house with lots of presents and decorations. We had the best parties then. But we also all have to grow up, and although we were close, it was when I started to have my own opinions that we began to drift apart.

My parents raised me the only way they knew how to raise a child, but it was brutal for me. Both families were cut from the same cloth; they were very cruel, manipulating, judgmental, and always out for themselves. I have forgiven my parents and I miss them, but I don't miss the drama that came with them when they were alive.

And my own life choices took its toll on my family. But it was finally over; I had my son and he was free from the life that I despised. I did not want him to be part of the world I grew up in. I wanted him raised to become what I thought a man should be, and to treat women with respect, to be a loyal and kind person, a young man able to make up his own mind and walk and partake in God's destiny for his life.

As a young child I dreamed of having a big family, a close-knit group to walk through all of life's ups and downs with. I knew life came with all of the roller coasters of joy and sadness. *I often wondered what a happy family was; I just knew mine was not one.* We had some happy times, but day to day it was rough. And of all the families I knew, none of them seemed happy. I thought a normal life meant one of love, kindness, and trust. Growing up in mob life is a horrible way to grow up—we see too much death, destruction, and despair. In that life, we grow up way too fast being a part of our parents' lives and the drama they create by their choices and destiny. I didn't have a choice when I was told to do something by my parents; they expected it to be done. There were no ifs, ands, or butts allowed, ever—my opinion did not count.

My parents should have shielded me from all of the violence on the street as well as from what they brought into our home from the "business." Or talking about, at the breakfast table, who was "whacked" the night before . . . only to find out it was my friend's father and brother who I had been hanging out with the night before in their home! They were found dead while going out for Sunday breakfast. *Growing up in a heartless, cruel, and abusive world, I became just as they were.*

As a child I started as a blank slate. What I learned from my parents and their examples of how they treated and cared for each other—or didn't do so—this is how I thought it was supposed to be. How I was treated during my early years shaped me into who I was to be in years to come. I did not like the person I was at times, but I did not know how to change myself. Little did I know I couldn't change myself without a relationship with God! I had to give up control of my life and give over my will to his will for me.

Parents are supposed to nurture and guide our young minds and hearts so that we will grow up to be honest, work hard, get married, have a family, and live happily ever after.

But what if you're taught to be deceptive and learn what it means to be in the "family"—with secrets and poker faces always the norm—and no matter how unhappy at home you are, you must put on a brave front with a happy face for the outside world to see? Whatever I heard at home stayed at home. *If my father heard any part of his business on the street, I would face grave consequences. I was taught never to tell the secrets from home to anyone—ever.*

When my parents passed I came to grips with being alone—all alone. No immediate contacts to call for help, no loved ones to call, just problems. No one left to count on. But there was God.

After my father passed I began to have a relationship with my sister mentioned in an earlier chapter.

So I will call my father's daughter PC. My Aunt was my father's sister. As a child I spent many Christmas dinners at her home. Auntie put on a spread and decorated every inch of her home; that kept us kids busy for hours looking at it all. Trains and animated dolls, the music . . . it was all like being at the North Pole with Santa.

My Aunt came into my life again after my parents passed. We had not spoken to each other due to an issue in the past, and we were not close as I grew up. And suddenly we would talk to each other for hours by phone, as she did not travel long distances anymore. Auntie lived in the same neighborhood as when she was married back in the '50s. A couple of times I went to visit my sister at her home in New York, and she came to visit me in South Carolina as well. During a trip to New York to see my sister, we decided to go visit Auntie who had never seen us together as children. My sister was in her sixties and I was in my forties by the time of this visit. This was the first time we would all be together, decades after being kept apart. It was a wonderful event. Auntie was so happy to see us both together, and all issues from the past finally came to an end. This would be our only visit as Auntie became very ill and passed not long after, and so did my long-lost sister. She died from an aneurysm after returning from a trip to Africa.

My way of thinking about everything was from a defensive mode. My brain defaulted to go off at the least sign of trouble. Panic mode would set in immediately. I would cry and pace my home and wonder how I was going to get out of the latest situation in my life. But I had survived all of the past issues I faced, so I knew I would get through this as well.

I kept asking God to make me self-sufficient—what a joke that was—and selfish. We need to be sufficient in the Lord—He will provide for us. We cannot make it through any troubled times without Him carrying us through.

Eighteen

Learning to Depend on Jesus

I called the girl I worked with several years earlier to see if an opening for a logistics dispatcher was available in her company. I had worked in the transportation industry before, and I knew I could make a good living. After talking to the owner of the company and getting an interview, I was hired in 2006. Once I started, all was great. Money was flowing in and I enjoyed the people I worked with. Life was good.

Then it happened: BAM! My son had an accident in 2008. On the Friday after Thanksgiving, he was at a red light waiting to turn left when a car hit him from behind and spun his car into oncoming traffic, where he was hit again. It seems my life is on a roller coaster all of the time, with just a few breaks for normal life in between. My son called me after he came to a stop in the median. I will never forget running out in my sweats to drive to North Charleston, where he was waiting after the accident. When I arrived at the scene, not many people were there; not even the cops were on the scene when I arrived. My son was badly shaken. Once the police officer arrived he began to talk to all the people who were involved with the accident—everyone but my son. You would think if you are hit from behind waiting at a red light it is the other person's fault. But not in this case. The cop talked to the pizza delivery driver who hit my son first; the pizza driver told the officer that my son pulled out in front of him, which was not evident by the colors of paint from the cars that hit the van my son was driving. The people driving another car hit my son in the side door; he had been thrown into oncoming traffic as a result of being hit in the back of the van, which sent him spinning. These people did not speak English when I asked what happen. They did not seem to have registration, nor did they have a license or insurance on them.

I tried to talk to the officer, but he wanted no part of what I had to say. Instead I am listening to this cop telling the pizza driver and the other drivers—who all of a sudden spoke good English—that the pizza driver was not at fault. I couldn't believe what I was hearing.

I was trying to speak with the officer after I heard his comments, to understand what really happened. I tried to show him the paint marks on our vehicle to prove who hit who and where. The police report was written so that my son was listed as the one who caused the accident. I tried to contact the officer and talk about the scene and accident. I talked to the judge at the hearing after the accident. The officer had the pizza delivery driver listed as a state witness.

This was one of the hardest times in my life, seeing my son hurting through all of this. I could not go to work for weeks after the accident; my son was in so much pain he had to have emergency surgery five days after the accident. During his holiday break from college my son had a CAT-scan to see if his sinuses where closed up because he was having the same issues he had as a child with his sinus cavities. This caused so much pressure in his nasal cavities that he would have terrible headaches. Because of his already swollen sinuses, the accident caused so much pressure on his brain and face. They had to schedule surgery to repair his nose, open his sinuses, and relieve the pressure caused by the injuries he had when he hit his face on the steering wheel and window during the collisions with the other cars. The surgery lasted five and a half hours. It was the longest time in my life, waiting for him to come out of surgery; once again I was alone to deal with it all. My son was out of it for two months; he suffered with pain, migraines, and vertigo. I could not go to work and leave him alone.

Waiting the few days for my son's surgery, I started to break down and cry out to God for help. It was at this very moment I realized I could not protect my son out in the world. I gave my son to the God I had been praying to my whole life. *God gave me my son and God had to look out for him; I could not do it anymore.* Night after night I sat and talked to God and prayed for help for my to son to be OK. I was working from home during this time since I didn't have anyone to come stay at my home while my son recuperated.

My new company of three years fired me after Christmas. I heard a voice in my spirit telling me what they were doing, so I began trying to get another company to hire me before I was fired. Again, I had to protect my son and myself and try to provide for us.

Now I had a sick and hurting child, I was out of a job with no money for medication or food, it was Christmas, and I was beside myself with worry. I talked to a trucking company in New Jersey that I used to run my truck-loads. I explained what was going on and they agreed to take me on. They made a bundle off me from the past two years and knew I was successful in the industry, so they agreed to take me on if my boss did fire me. He did and I left feeling a bit betrayed as I was a good worker for them, came in early, left late, and worked at home all hours of the night. I was on commission sales and had to hustle to make a thousand a week. What no one knew is that I was becoming weaker. I finally broke down and went to the doctor. I was in denial of my aches and pains because I didn't have time to be sick. *What I mean is I'm stubborn, and I would not give in to the idea that I could be incapacitated and not able to work and take care of my son and myself.* My doctor ran all the tests for the several different issues I was having. Now I was left to wait for the results.

My son needed medication and I was running out of savings. It took two months for my son to recover enough to go back to college. He was loved and had great friends and teachers at college. Finally, someone showed some compassion toward us. The school let him make up all of his work that he had missed so he could complete his courses. He was allowed to return and start his new classes with the understanding that he also had to complete his previous semester.

To say his life was hard is an understatement. He was sick, and God put great friends in his life through this time. By the grace of God he made it through to continue on to finish his education. He graduated with a B.A. in Music Education in 2012. My son loves teaching the younger children; he is a big kid himself. The classes he taught during his internship showed him he could make a difference in young minds and lives, just as Chuck had made one in his life so many years earlier. It just takes one teacher to change the course of a child's life with such positive influence and love. But as with all good things, music education jobs were cut from most schools, and he decided to launch out with his talent to make a living.

Meanwhile, *I was becoming more incapacitated by the many different auto-immune diseases that were destroying my body.* Lupus; Raynaud's—a circulatory disease that left my hands and feet cold and blue with white spots; GERD (gastro esophageal reflux disease, in which the acid burns holes in the throat and esophagus) . . . I struggled with all of these. I was always burping acid, a horrible condition. Fibromyalgia, which causes a pain all over the body and has many symptoms because the nerve endings are always on fire, almost like a rapid fire—I had this also. It would be so painful to touch my skin in the areas that were flaring up; even wearing clothes hurt as it rubbed against and put pressure on my skin. Rheumatoid arthritis and Osteo arthritis made my life a living hell. It led to so much swelling and pain that led to bones being pushed out of my body and deforming my hands, fingers, and right ankle. The most painful time was when my right ankle started to grow a bone out the side of my flat anklebone. This pain would never stop and would keep me awake and crying out for God to heal me.

My legs swelled up to balloon size, to the point that I could press on my ankle and leave a very deep depression of the skin. I was told this was "4-plus" edema. Sometimes I could not bend my legs from the amount of water in them. My feet would jingle on the top as I walked, and this was very uncomfortable; my long toes were mere stubs out of the front of my feet. My skin felt as if it would rip and explode. My hands were very weak from the progressive attack of arthritis in my entire body.

I also suffered with bleeding ulcerative colitis, which left me with severe abdominal pain. I suffered with this since childhood due to the violence in my family that I kept inside. This condition plagued me throughout life, until my fifties. After cancer I would not do hormones because I kept my diet healthy and knew what not to do to keep from inflaming my body. My vitamin D was so low and not producing well in my body, to the point that my hair fell out and my fingernails and bones became brittle and weak. My muscles deteriorated to the point where my shoulders would pop out of their sockets; to this day I have the chiropractor punch them back in when they pop out. Strengthening my muscles helps this, but it wasn't an option at the time. I had to go on fifty thousand milligrams a week in order to combat the symptoms of the illness, as the medication is like a hormone more than just a mere vitamin. My level was as low as 11 at one point; now it is in the 40s.

It all came to a head one day as I stepped off the sidewalk into the street. As I was walking my legs quit; they just gave out. And I was on the ground wondering what the heck happened. I had been in denial way too long and all of the above issues led to still more issues, and before I knew it I was fighting for my life. The pain was so intense I began to see a rheumatologist. She was an amazingly compassionate woman who saw the pain I was in and tried to halt the progression of deformity beginning to happen in my hands, feet, and body.

After I began treatment I was on 38 medications a day, including supplements and vitamins, some to offset the side effects of all of the meds. Some days I could not get out of bed. If it were not for my dogs, which needed to be walked, I never would have walked out of the house. I kept it all to myself as I was on my own and my son was in college and I know he would quit and come home to care for me if I had asked. I was not going to be a burden on him and halt his path in life for my sake. I was told I was going to be crippled in ten years if we could not stop the forward progression of these illnesses. I was getting shots in both shoulders and hips to numb the pain so I could get through life. With all of the meds I was so goofy and forgetful I was not myself, and I became angry and begged the Lord to help me. I think I was so far down from who I was that I was willing to give up to someone—anyone—to care for me. I was so tired of fighting. I was ready to let God come in and take care of me. I was tired of the memories, and of lying in bed for so long that you have nothing to do but think and cry. *During this time I went into depression because of the constant pain and lack of sleep.* I felt everyone's life would be better off without me as I was losing my hope that these illnesses would ever end.

My son was now in his second year of college. I was alone and sick; the pain from the rheumatoid arthritis was excruciating as this bone continued to push its way out of my ankle. Once again I decided I was going to check out, and this time I would get it right.

One night I was sitting on the edge of my bed, talking out loud and complaining about the pain and what my life had become. I was angry and bitter, as I once had a completely different thought as to how my life would look. Up to this point, all of my plans were dying off quickly. *Even though I have always talked out loud to myself to hash out my issues, I was now hoping I was actually talking to the Lord* —otherwise, I was nuts. Sometimes I also hear Satan trying to fill my heart and mind with his negative lies. Then I heard in my spirit: *You're going to die, or else where is your God with all of the pain you have?* And I said to myself: *He's not healing me because of the things I have done in my past.* I know my past, and so does Satan. So I had to learn to cast his evil thoughts out, to fill my mind with the Word of God and know that a loving God would not say those things to me. *Doubt is the biggest killer of faith. When trials and tribulation came I would always default back to my original mind-set before I was saved.* Because I was newly saved I had to learn to choose what I would let my mind listen to: the negative reminders from my past, or would I choose to listen to the positive words of God?

I think the hardest time I had in my walk was believing that when Jesus died to save me from my sins it was *finished*, over, and I was washed clean of all of my sins and accepted into a pure and loving family. My mind was still living in the past with all I had done.

Flashbacks from different occasions often would enter my day, and these would trigger another conversation with my invisible God. I hoped He was listening to me all of the time. I was a doubter; all of the conversations to this point, and I was still wondering if I was truly talking to God or if I was going nuts. I had a really hard time believing because of the thoughts in my mind and the horrible memories I had. Although I was saved and made a new person, I had to *choose* life and leave the death of who I was behind me.

Then came the time when the soft voice I was unsure of became stern within me—it was strongly against something I was talking about doing to myself in my anger and pain. As I dealt with all of the illnesses the pain became unbearable, and I began to think of killing myself again. I was so angry it was hard to feel God's love. I was feeling dark and gloomy and wondered if I was going to become crippled from the arthritis. I went through these illnesses for five years with days and nights of waves of pain that never seamed to end. I just wanted all of the pain and struggling to end. In the height of my rantings I began to think of the pros of death and why it made sense for me to take my life. I was ramping myself up in anger.

I was having a meltdown in pain and then I heard it: "Do you think you are worth less to me than the dust I created you from? I breathed life into you." I felt like my Father in Heaven had just yelled at me to shock me out of my fit of rage because of my situation. For the next few hours the voice of the Lord told me I had to forgive the three people who had hurt me most in life. We battled over this because I did not want to forgive them. I heard in my spirit: *I cannot forgive your sins if you don't forgive those who have sinned against you.*

Even though by this point I had said the sinner's prayer and been baptized, I still didn't know what the true meaning of having a relationship with the living Christ was all about. But I knew I had to begin my journey to choose life and overcome all the adversity in my life. I didn't have anyone who loved the Lord to talk to. I had to learn it all on my own, with God's guidance and love. Today I'm so thankful I had this completely alone time with God, and I feel lucky to have had Him as my teacher. I thought all his people heard Him as I did, but boy was I wrong. Those staunch Christians who did not hear from Him as I did became upset with me.

When I stepped out in faith to accept Jesus into my life, I had to begin the process of forgiving all those who hurt me in my past. I had not repented fully of every sin in my life; some I didn't remember, but some I chose to forget. But God knows every sin I had in me, and I had to remember them, talk them over with Him, ask Him to forgive me, and then forget them because God forgot them the minute I asked Him to forgive me! I had to learn to forgive myself, and that was not easy!

When I was down I would hear songs that are now my go-to songs, those I turn to when I need lifting up. *The one song that changed the way I looked at myself was called "Beautiful," by MercyMe.* I heard in my spirit, while listening to it on the radio: *This is my song for you.* I listened to it over and over once I understood all the words. *I started to cry when I realized God had just told me I was beautiful.* I did not feel beautiful: my hair was gone, my face was ashen gray and wrinkled; I didn't even recognize myself anymore. And yet, I began to feel the love of Jesus and the grace he gives us every day. I had to learn what grace really means before I could relax and stop trying so hard to do the right thing so I would have a secure place in Heaven. I've learned that grace is a gift from God and there is not one blessed good work I can do to earn it. All I can do is believe in what Jesus has done for me on the cross. *I now know the difference between religion and relationship. Religion is man trying to work his way into Heaven by reaching up to God to accept Him.*

In reality, God is heartbroken, as his creation has rejected Him. He loves us so much and wants us not to be lost and end up in hell forever. God would not force us to love and worship Him because forced love is no real love at all. Instead, we must choose to grab his hand and let Him guide us into his will for our lives.

To guarantee all his people would have an opportunity to bring themselves back into his loving arms, God sent his Son, Jesus, who became the last sacrifice for man's sins—forever. By sending his Son to become the atonement for all of our sins—past, present, and future—with this **last** sacrifice of a pure lamb, Jesus, God took the ultimate step. God knew Jesus would obey and go through with his sacrifice and not back out when He saw how hard it would be. Jesus knew what was going to happen to Him and subjected himself to the pain to come anyway. Why? Because He knew it would save us from death. God had to pour out all of his wrath on his Son instead of us. And this is because we cannot stop sinning, no matter how hard we try. God knew that Jesus would not give in to the temptation of Satan to sell out just to get out of completing the painful and horrific mission that his Father commissioned for Him once and for all.

There was only one way to do this, and it was the Lord's way, and that is to accept that Jesus came to this earth to be betrayed, condemned to death on the cross by crucifixion, killed, placed in the tomb, and then raised to life on the third day. Jesus rose and then ascended to the right hand of the Father. As we accept this fact in our hearts, we too are born again. Our old mind-sets and sinful hearts are made brand new and we get a second chance for a new and everlasting life with God.

I became obsessed with knowing God. Of learning all of his teachings and finding out just who Jesus really is, not what others say, but what God says about his Son.

I have many evangelists the Lord used to teach me and confirm all we spoke about, and these good people kept my faith growing. We will be learning— until we take our last breath—what the Word of God in the New Testament really means. The Bible is not a book of harsh judgment, but one of great love and forgiveness. I knew that if I could just tap that love I would know what real love felt like, and I would never be alone again.

Insomnia kept me up at night; I just could not shut my brain off from all the worry about the situations I was in. I found that if I put TBN's *Praise the Lord* show on throughout the night, listening to Paul Crouch reading and talking about Scriptures all night long, it began to seep into my mind and I would fall asleep. And now I found myself sleeping through the nights more. There was this great desire to accept the love of the Lord and escape the evil I was raised in and wanted out of because of the drama always around me. I was ready to change and find true happiness, peace, joy, and most of all, love. I wanted to love and be loved. I had so much love to give, but felt like no one wanted it.

In February 2009, my ex-roommate asked me if his friend could move in temporarily; she needed a place for a while. I said OK. Her name is Cecilia and she knew the Bible inside and out, and it was during this time the Lord had been working on me to learn his words and, through them, I would find healing and the answers I had been looking for concerning my past and my future. Every day, the words I kept hearing were: *Have faith and patience*, and *Have the faith of a mustard seed*. Heck, I didn't even know what a mustard seed was!

At first, when Cecilia moved, in we were two strong personalities living together, but after the both of us did some beating of our chests for independence, we became friends. It was good to have someone I could go to when I had a question. God would tell me something I did not understand, and I would ask Cecilia and she would help me find the answer I needed.

Cecilia and I were roommates for a while when she asked me if I wanted to come to her church. I heard the Lord say go, so I went. But truthfully, I was not into churches anymore. So much rejection and too many hypocritical and judgmental people in these "houses of God" that I had run to for help earlier in life. I was turned away many times due to not having money for the collection plate; I was very poor and did not have the fancy clothes that others wear to church. Plus I had two tattoos and was looked at as a low-life kind of person. Here I was looking to find the Lord in his house, and all I found were cliques, gossip, and shunning of those who were different, instead of acceptance.

But I took the chance, trusted the Lord, and honored his request of me to go to Cecilia's church. It was a Baptist church and very plain compared to the ornate Catholic churches I had been raised in. It felt comfortable; as Cecilia knew everyone, I was accepted. So I asked God, "Why here? Why this church, Lord? There's nothing but a cross and crown of thorns on it." I heard, clear as a bell in my spirit: *Because I am here.* That was all I needed to hear, so I stayed.

I tried to make friends, but people were not very accepting in the beginning. I kept going, however, because I knew the Lord wanted me to go. I sat by myself, like a leper, and a short time later a few people came over and introduced themselves. I dove into these new friendships and the church itself; I became a member and volunteered at the recreational center one day a week. I went in at 11 a.m. and stayed to 3 p.m. most days, and to 6 p.m. when they were short-staffed. My job was checking in members to play basketball or work out in the gym.

I began to go to the classes that I needed to be baptized and understand what it means to take this step in faith and grow in my walk with the Lord. I was baptized in February 2009. I knew one thing was for certain when I made the appointment for my baptism: I *did not know* what would happen to me by taking this step toward the Lord. But I *did know* that I was so excited at taking this step. I had proclaimed the sinner's prayer and dedicated my life and the life of my son to Him. Little did I know that once I gave my heart and went under the water, my whole life would change in an instant. I went into the water as a sinner; I came up in God's family, and I felt the difference immediately. I had a conscience for the first time in my life; I was feeling guilty about everything I had done in my past. This is where the work began in my life to start my walk with Jesus.

The best part of this story is the day I made the appointment to be baptized. Cecilia and I were talking about my excitement to be baptized, and told her I wished my son would dedicate his life to Jesus too. Just as the words left my lips, the phone rang: it was my son.

At college he had met a great young man who had invited him to go to church, and here he met a great group of people. He was calling to tell me he had accepted Jesus as his Lord and Savior and was going to be baptized. He was worried I would be upset! Wow, how the Lord works. Upset? I was over the moon. We were joining the Lord's family together! He was at college and I was here at home. God is everywhere, and He knows what needs to be done in every one of us. This was what I had dreamed for my son when we ran away, and here it was all coming together. Praise the Lord!

When I started this journey with Jesus I was really a blank slate; I did not have any preconceived ideas of a relationship with Jesus. As I have said, as a child I loved my statue of Jesus; it gave me peace when all hell would break loose in my home. Today, I say my prayers in the morning and go about my day. I talk to Jesus all day long about everything—even something like a parking space I need to be close to a store if I'm in pain and it's hard to walk far.

I have now been on my own, without a significant other in my life, for 15 years. I made such horrible choices I just wanted to heal and be alone to search my heart to learn what is it I do that keeps making the same choices in men. I have had a date here and there, but I have decided to be on my own, as I've come to realize I have made the same mistakes in all the men I've met. There has to be more to love and marriage that I need to learn before I dive into another mistake—more than just "not wanting to be alone." God will bring the right one, or I would rather stay alone than be in a godless marriage void of true love, trust, and respect. I was becoming a woman of God, strong in whom I belonged to. I was happy to be home alone, learning and spending time talking to Jesus.

I was so excited about giving my life to the Lord that I wanted to share my past and all I had been delivered from. I typed up the whole sordid story and I gave it to the pastor to read. Watching him read my story . . . well, he became horrified, and his whole demeanor changed. He looked at me in fear and/or horror—I could not tell which! Then he said I could come and talk, but he did not think I should tell my story yet.

I realized once I was home he had been horrified by my story, and that he hadn't been seeking understanding. After talking it all over with the Lord that night, He told me what happened was the pastor had judged me. As time passed, I was still going to this church, but people started to stay away from me. The few who *were* friendly were not talking to me; they would say hello and move on. The pastor stopped coming to shake my hand during the greeting. It seems that he told his friends what my life had contained, and they now thought I was the plague. So all of the phony "Praise the Lord!"s and "I surrender my heart to God!"—these were all bogus. I came home and cried out to God. I was certain I was done with churches for good. I told Jesus I wanted to know his truth—not a man's or a pastor's or even a church's, but *his* truth. After this I did not want to even read the Bible because a man had decided what to put in it and what not to put in it. How would I know if it was the truth? I just knew that I needed Jesus himself more than ever.

If I was going to dedicate my life to an entity I could not see, I wanted the truth from Jesus and not from some wannabe representative who was a bad stand-in for a loving, forgiving, and most of all accepting God.

Meanwhile, Cecilia had found a place of her own and had moved out to start her new life. But in the end, we both had gained a new friendship.

I dove into finding out the truth about *this Jesus* on my own, and I began talking to him directly. Days passed and I continued to learn all I could about Jesus through his teaching and many other pastors I was led to listen to on TV. I still went to church for God, but no one talked to me anymore, and the friends I made were gone, except for a few. *All throughout my life I had learned to ignore those around me by shielding myself from judgment.* I was not in the church for friends, although it would have been nice, but God had asked me here. And because of that, I told myself, I belonged.

After having a dream about Pete I will call him for this part of the story— the young man whom I met years earlier when he came to live with me and followed my path to Folly Beach years—I thought the Lord wanted me to find him and help him, so I did. When I found him he was in jail, and he had three children with his girlfriend. This girl was questionable in character, but I thought I could help them all by showing love; after all, I was Jesus' person now, right? What could go wrong? Well, it did—and so goes the next disaster in my story.

After seeing Pete, his girl, and their three adorable toddlers, I felt bad for them, and they did not have a place to live. I had cared about Pete since he was 15. Although his life was hard, it was so by his choice, and his issues had kept him in drama all of the time, simply struggling to survive. Now he was a grown-up and had kids of his own. I fell in love with his kids; they were sweet. But my heart broke because they were abused and afraid. I knew I had to give them peace in their lives, if only for a while. I thought if I moved them into my home the abuse they were facing would stop. They were so young and high-strung with fear. I took them in to live with me and brought them all to my church, where they were baptized after several months of attending church and becoming members. The young man needed some serious advice and help from God. I told him to go talk to one of the pastors in the church I was baptized in, to get advice, and this would help Pete find help on how to deal with his inner demons. I never thought the pastor would not help him find his path to God. After all, he was the pastor, he was a father of two young children himself, and he was there to lead the flock and help people with their issues, right? Wrong again.

Well, he did not help him. Once again a representative of the Lord was not right with himself, so how could he help this young man? The pastor drew his children away from them as they watched the kids' class during service. Now these two parents, Pete and his girl, were so very far from the Lord, but they nonetheless dove into it, seeking guidance. When they felt comfortable, they participated in all the events at church with their children. Their life was turning for good for the first time in a long time. But when the pastor and the rest of the church shunned them, Pete left rejected and angry, and once again I lost my love for this church.

I had been scheduled to give my testimony during a basketball game, as had several others. I gave my paper to another pastor who worked in the gym to read over before I would speak to the crowd at the game. I heard the Lord, in my spirit tell me to get the paper back; they will shun you and judge you so harshly, my spirit said. So I walked in to speak to another pastor, one who I had been a little friendly with, and asked him for the paper I had turned in for approval before speaking. When he asked why, I told him what the Lord had told me.

I saw in his face he was shocked at my past, but he had more class and chose not to shun me to my face, as the head pastor had. What was more shocking was the look on his face when I told him that the Lord told me this congregation would judge me harshly. It confirmed that he knew it was true, and relief showed on his face when I said I was not going to give my testimony.

I did tell the head pastor what I thought, God forgive me. I told him that because he grew up as a pastor's son he had never seen the horrific side of life I had been describing. That as a representative of God he should have an understanding that not everyone has had a safe life. And that I felt, truthfully, that he should not be serving as a pastor. The church eventually split, and a new pastor came in and others in the congregation left and started a new church.

Most of the churches I have visited in the past had a harsh judgment of those people who didn't look like them or appeared poorer than most. I went to hear God's words for comfort, and all I received was the false doctrine of religion and the theologies of men who were in pastoral positions who must not have known who Jesus was! Why do I say this? They never spoke his name once during the sermons! I was not inclined to listen to man's lies anymore; I wanted the real truth.

Even after Pete and his girlfriend were baptized, the evil was too strong in both of them. They lived with me for eight months, but things went wrong in their lives.

During the time Pete and his family lived with me I had a few sinus surgeries. I was left alone by them; they rarely asked if I needed anything. After healing up, there was some violence between us, and this became unbearable in my home. I felt I had to sleep with one eye open.

The Lord has used all of this to give me wisdom and discernment. Now I can see the evil in people and I know who to be wary of. Thank you, Lord!

Nineteen

A New Beginning

I will say as I trusted many different people to live with me through the years, some items would come up missing. I've learned not to be so trusting. One thing that came up missing was photographs of famous boxers who were friends of my father in his youth. There was one of my father and Frank Sinatra—before the singer became famous—attending a baseball game together. At one point I was told it appraised for a few thousand dollars.

God was in control of my world and life moves on, and one day as I went to the town post office I had a feeling I needed to go visit my friend who owned a hardware store next to the post office on Folly Beach. We had been friends for a long time, and I would go in and sit and visit her when business was slow. As I pulled in to the post office parking lot, I saw how busy the store was, with so many cars in the parking lot, and I decided not to go in.

As I was back in the van leaving the lot, I clearly heard the Lord tell me to go inside her store. I have a bad habit of not listening sometimes, but as I drove home to my community and came down the driveway to my gate, *I heard the Lord scream at me: "GO BACK NOW!" So I said OK, turned around, headed back to the store, and walked inside.* As I entered the store my friend and her working staff looked up as if to say, "I cannot talk now.

We are slammed!" I nodded and stood out of the workers' and customers' way as it was a small shop filled to the brim with product. About five minutes after I had walked into the store, a gentleman walked in asking if anyone knew a property manager; he had two homes he needed help caring for. He was not happy with the rental company he had been using. It was like slow motion in school: I raised my hand and said . . . "I am a property manager." . . . He asked if we could talk and later offered me the position, which lasted seven years. *The point is God leads us to where we need to be when he puts an opportunity in our path.* If we listen to him, we can have it, and if not it will be offered to someone who will listen.

There are so many stories of provision, healing, and opportunity since the day I took Jesus seriously and surrendered my life to Him.

Living on Folly Beach, there is only one road in and out. One day as I was passing the little church just off the island I had passed many times daily for a long time, I began hearing a soft voice: "Go in there." I did not feel comfortable going inside, so I did not obey the Lord. Over a period of two years I kept hearing "Go in there." Until one day I heard it loud and clear: *"GO IN NOW!"* Once again, I had been reluctant until the Lord, in a loud, clear voice, yelled at me to turn around and "Go in now!" Well, with summer traffic to the beach making U-turns or getting back into the line of traffic, this was not an easy feat. I finally made it into the parking lot. I made my way inside, and just three people were there, for noonday prayers. The pastor was a small man with a big anointing. I felt happy when I walked in this church. I started walking toward the altar, and the closer I got I began to cry and cry, more and more, and then I was sobbing, and I did not know why.

I went to the church daily for a week or so, and then they had a huge revival. I had never been to a Southern AME revival, and I have to say I became Pentecostal that day. As a Roman Catholic, we were not allowed to make a peep in church. Here, when I saw people running around the church full of the Holy Spirit, I thought they were nuts, and I wanted to run out! Then something amazing happened; the church filled to capacity. They had an altar call for anyone wanting to have the Holy Spirit come into them, and I found myself getting up and walking over to the head pastor leading the service. He asked me what I wanted God to do for me, and my response was that I wanted Jesus to give me the gift of the Holy Spirit.

Well, the next thing I knew two elderly ladies were hugging me and yelling, "You've been slain!" and they were picking me up off the floor. I had no idea what the heck that meant, much less understanding all of what had just happened. I was told that I had been imbued with the Holy Spirit of Jesus. I felt like I wanted to run around the church! I was full of tingling energy like I had never felt before. Happiness, joy, and peace is all I was feeling, and for the first time in my life. It was so awesome I did not want it to end, so I kept coming back to this church. I was slain three more times in different churches.

The only issue was, after the revival I realized this pastor had not had a congregation for a very long time. I began to wonder why God had me come here. It all became clear three Sundays later, after going to this church, when an older couple came forward to give their testimony. Little did I know that this meeting would completely alter the course of my life—I would never be the same.

During this Sunday service people were giving their testimonies of all the miracles the Lord had given them. *A couple named David and Barbara came up, stood at the pulpit together, and gave their testimonies of healings* from cancer, paraplegia, shingles, and many other illnesses they had suffered from during their lives together. And all of these had been healed through prayers and speaking the Word—all with one touch from God. As I watched them speak I saw an aura of white light around them, and I heard the Lord say, "You need to meet these two people." After they were finished, I tried to meet them. I walked up to David to meet him and shake his hand and he looked me in my eyes and said that I have "unrecognized authority" from the Lord. *Really?* Because all I knew was that for the last few years I had been struggling with many illnesses and had been taking many medications to try to halt their progression. He looked shocked but went on to shake other hands. I wanted to get David and Barbara's number so I could talk with him more, but that day it was not meant to be.

The following Sunday, however, they came to the church again, and this time they were sitting behind me. I asked for their number and told them what I had seen and been told about them by the Lord.

On my first visit to their home, David and I talked for hours; the time just seemed to fly by. I told both David and Barbara everything that was going on in my life. It was then David told me of a vision pertaining to my irritable bowel issue. It was during this time that David and Barbara laid hands on my stomach and prayed for it to be healed. I was a bit taken back, as I have never believed in healings. I really thought most of the people were planted when these "healings" occurred on television.

But we had a great day and I went home. That night I was in horrors as my stomach had so much pain and cramping. I had no idea what was going on.

Later that evening, I started to feel like there was a python in my stomach! Needless to say, the prayers had started the peristaltic muscles in my bowels working again. After years of bleeding, ulcerative colitis, and irritable bowel syndrome, I went into remission, and the flare-ups are now under control! I have to eat right and drink fluids, but we all have to care for our bodies if we want them to function correctly.

This was the beginning of many healing miracles in my life. David and his family took me under their wing and began to teach me who I was in the Lord. David and I would talk for hours, and I could listen to him speak and never get bored. He had a direct link to the Holy Spirit. He would call me with words from the Lord every morning and, surprisingly, he was always dead on as to what the Lord was telling me, so it was a confirmation of all I was being taught.

The years passed, and I was being taught what it meant to take Jesus into my heart. What my relationship with the Lord was, and what my purpose in life was all about.

David was a renaissance man and a master craftsman. David and Barbara were born and raised in England. Their lives and stories are so amazing, to hear the lives they have lived. David was a genius inventor, artist, and his talents were so vast I could not put them all in words. Among other things, David and his family built a 100-foot-tall ship and sailed all over Canada and the East Coast down to Florida and beyond. But the greatest assignment David lived out was his walk with Jesus. *David never pretended to be anything other than himself—not perfect, but very loved by Jesus. His example taught me to stop being hard on myself for my mistakes,* and to ask God to forgive me and help me move on and not do the same things again. *He uncomplicated the love of our Father and taught me how to be strong, to realize that God had a plan for my life.* He taught me love and kindness and showed me the encouragement I never had in life. He told me when I was wrong and helped me understand how a loving God works in our lives. We can talk to Jesus from right where we are; no intercessor is needed.

At this point in my life I was walking with Jesus and learning to shed the old; I was beginning to move forward as I was being changed from the inside out. As I read the Word of God, He was softening my heart to be all that He wants me to be.

I met David and Barbara when I was on my own with God and still learning the destiny He has for my life. Having the friendship of this family, I finally felt part of something wonderful. Throughout my life I never felt I belonged anywhere. The way David explained it to me is that God's people are not accepted everywhere. This does not have to leave me feeling hurt, as Jesus also was shunned and persecuted because of who He was.

My love for God shows through me, and some people are uncomfortable with me around. I never saw or felt the Lord emanating out of me until one day in the church. I was sitting there reading the Bible when someone came to ask me a question and then told me, "The light of God is in your eyes." It shocked me; I had to run to the mirror to see what it looked like, as I never saw that in my eyes! Today I can recognize the light of the Lord in my eyes as Jesus has had me look in the mirror during some of my teaching, just for confidence. *When the Lord wants me to see myself as He sees me, I look. Our Lord is always with us, inside of us; He never leaves even when we think He is not there.* We are the ones who move away from Him. If we ask Him into our hearts He never leaves us, no matter what we do. If we ask for forgiveness and repent for what we did or said, we know He is working on us. We would never give his love and concern a thought before we asked Him into our hearts; we now have the knowledge of the love of God and we cannot even fathom someone loving us in the times we are wrong.

The holidays came during our first year of friendship. My son and I were invited go to David and Barbara's family for Thanksgiving and Christmas dinners. *I have to say that first Thanksgiving I felt as though I was dining with the Waltons!* No one was fighting, no one was drunk and arguing in the yard, and everyone was happy and joking. It was amazing to see a family enjoying each other's company for the holidays. My family dinners always ended with a family fight or an argument, which led to the shunning of certain family members until one caved in and apologized even if they were not wrong. I never knew families could actually have this much fun together! In my family, we were always running away from one another, and there was often a grudge held against someone else.

And then a pastor came in to my life, a man named Andre. He came into my life when David's son Stephen held a prayer meeting for all of us who had issues needing a touch from God, and who needed the enjoyment of the fellowship with friends and family. Andre has been very influential in my walk because he has clarified for me just what a relationship with Jesus is. It is not complicated; it's filled with the love of a Father who did not come to judge his people but to free them from their sins. Andre has been all over the world doing the Lord's work. His simplified explanation of Scripture makes it easy for me to learn and absorb the Bible and his teachings. During many of his visits over the years Andre has had instruction for me from the Lord, words that would always confirm what the Lord and I were talking about.

Andre is a true man of God; his countenance when he comes into a room is evident as the Holy Spirit walks with him, and peace fills the room as he enters. Meetings led by him can last hours, and still no one wants to go home. Several times through the years Andre would call me in the morning with an anointed word that the Holy Spirit gave to him for me. I always enjoy a word from God, as we all have those times where we have to move forward for the answers we seek. But most of all there are the lessons we must learn in order to spiritually grow in our relationship with Jesus: faith and patience are the keys.

It was during Christmas Day dinner 2011 that *David popped up from the table and proclaimed, "Let's all lay hands on Rosanne for healing from all of the illnesses!"* I was a little nervous, wondering what was about to happen. Would this really work and restore my body? I knew when they laid hands on my stomach that this was the first time anyone showed me the healing power of God. We have to believe that God can and will do this for us because He loves us.

Then something amazing happened as the ten people— including my son—had their hands on me and were praying. I felt warmth start to spread from my toes to the top of my head, a feeling encompassing my entire body. I was flat-out scared of what was happening and a little skeptical. Was this really happening to me? Who was I that God would heal me? But David said God is "no respecter of persons." He cares so much for us even if we are skeptical—just so He can prove to us that He is for real.

When they were finished praying I did not feel any different; I still had all of the pain and aches. I was so used to having all of the pain for so many years that I did not do anything different—until one particular day. It was January 9, 2012, shortly after those holidays. I provide cleaning services with crews that do the actual work. On this day we had an undocumented guest in one of the beach homes. I received a call from the property manager asking me when we were coming to clean the house. I called my son and the cleaners and put the call out for help to come quickly. Only one girl could come, and she was two hours away. So my son and I began to clean the house. I knew my help would be worthless due to my limitations and all I could not do . . . until I was in a glass shower and realized I was using my arms to clean the glass. My shoulders had always been popping out, and I could hardly care for myself much less clean a glass shower. I started yelling, and I bent down and was able to bend my knees! At that moment, I realized I was set free. *And the progression of the arthritis my doctor had feared would render me a cripple in the coming years had finally stopped.*

Once I felt better I knew I had to learn to understand the food and nutrients I was consuming. I began to juice fruits and vegetables to cleanse and detox my body as I began to wean off and rid my body of the toxins that had built up over the years from taking so many medications. I started to eat only organic and locally grown foods; I became a label reader! The food we eat today is not pure from chemicals and is turned into genetically modified food (GMO) in so much of the food we eat. My body was not able to digest the altered food being sold, and this was contributing to the diseases I suffered from. Once I cut out white sugar, high fructose corn syrup, and dozens of other chemicals processed in our foods, most of the non-organic food became off limits to me. I started to feel better and I was using juicing to help my immune system start back up. I was strengthening my cells by eating pure food.

David and his family helped me understand everything God has for me to learn in order to fulfill his destiny for my life. Jesus is real and He is the only one who can provide and heal us from all sickness and sin. If we give our lives to Him we will endure all of our tribulations with patience and grace, knowing that no matter what comes against us, Jesus will bring us through it all. No one is perfect when we love the Lord and choose to follow Him. We do not suddenly become holy on our own; it is by accepting the Holy Spirit, who dwells inside our hearts and teaches us in our daily routines what is right and wrong as we go about our lives.

When I met David and Barbara God knew I needed physical friends to care for me and help me understand. This time was for learning and growing. It was this family that taught me nothing is impossible when we *believe in* God, as He can do it all. The Lord, and my faith and belief in Him to take care of me and provide for all my finances and restore my health—well, God has done all these things. There is nothing I can do but have faith in Jesus and all He has done for me on the cross. By his physical stripes I was healed; by his death and resurrection I will live with Him in the kingdom of God. I have been given the gift of eternal life.

All of this is not to say I don't have issues; it means that every day they do not keep me in bed and out of reality all the time, like they used to! I am learning to live with who I am now and to stop thinking of how I was in the past—that is over and done. I thank God today for all I have been through. It makes me appreciate the days I feel great and have patience when all is not going smoothly in my life. *The best part is I do not fall apart anymore; I give it to Jesus and leave it with Him.* I am not in fear, worry, or stressed out, as I have seen his work in my life.

David was my best friend, mentor, encourager, and a true father figure, passed away in November 2013. I was brokenhearted, as I have lost many of the people I loved, and he was another who was gone to soon.

I was grieving his loss when I realized that my journey is just beginning and that David had been exactly what I needed to realize who I am in the Lord and how loved I am. God rest his soul, he is missed by many. David was an amazing man who was humble and loved the Lord so much. He was bringing souls home to the Lord from his hospital bed, until his death. Everyone he came across in the hospital had been touched by his love of the Lord, and most of the prophetic messages he spoke have come to pass except for a few, and I am looking forward to those coming to pass in the future. We are all better off for knowing this man of God, and this world is lucky to have had him. Today I am still a part of his family and have become close to Barbara. She has become a mother to me and her unconditional love is amazing and comforting. It's like when only a mother's love can make a bad day better. I've been grafted into a family, one that came with brothers and sisters. Praise the Lord!

Before David passed and my son left for Pennsylvania, my son gave his life to the Lord and was taken under God's wings. God has given amazing gifts to my son.

For my son's first acting job he was given the opportunity to perform with Sight & Sound Theater, one of the most God-centered theaters around, located in Lancaster, Pennsylvania. We had never heard of this place until God gave my son the opportunity to audition. He was there for 18 months and played Jesus at the end of a play during some performances. How amazing that God placed my son in his Son's shoes to walk in his thoughts and ways throughout the play. Ministering as Jesus at the end of the shows has changed my son for the rest of his life.

During the time of David passing, televangelist Paul Crouch passed away as well. Although he was on TV, his messages made him feel like a father figure to me from the first days I began watching TBN day and night. I lost these two great men in my life at about the same time. But God shows us He is still there and that we can persevere. God teaches us even through loss. Some people come into our lives in waves, some for a season, some for a reason, and some for a time. God ministers to us in so many different ways: through obedience, and through those he sends our way as mentors and teachers. If we are willing, he will help us grow through needed levels of faith to come into his destiny for our lives.

Twenty

Reflections of My Journey with Jesus

This chapter is not the end, but the beginning, of a journey. And even I do not know the path it is going down.

What an amazing past few years of miracles and growth in my walk with Jesus. I have learned to overcome what I'm faced with and believe all will work out for my good. After years of sickness and hair loss, today I am really happy to say my hair has started to grow back in! Getting rid of stress and giving all of my worries over to the Lord and trusting He will take care of it all—all of this has given me so much peace and serenity. As a woman on my own I had been worried about too many trivial issues, compared to all that God had given me, including freedom. Praise God!

Once every year I have diagnostic testing to see how my body is doing. I need to go and get tests done to see exactly what is going on in my body since everyone laid hands on me. I have my good days and bad days, but thanks to the Lord, I have more good than bad. Because some of the issues I have are hereditary, I have been extremely curious to see what the diagnostic tests will reveal. My father and mother both had heart and aneurysm issues. My sister had many aortic dissections all healed, except one; a thoracic aneurysm took her life, as it did my father. The evil one wanted me to be fearful and worried to the point that it would make me fretful. So I scheduled a round of tests for all of the areas I had been so ill in through the years.

The results were shocking, to say the least. All of the lesions on my esophagus, stomach, bowels, and colon were healed, with the exception of a small patch that has yet to heal fully. The irritable bowel is still present in my body, along with all fourteen autoimmune diseases. But they too are in remission as my immune system has kicked back in and my body is fighting for me to be well once again. I have flare ups but I believe in my full restoration! There are scars on my internal organs from all the years of suffering. *My stress test results showed my heart is strong and there are no signs of aneurysms. The Lord has known about my conditions since the onset of my relationship with Him,* and I fully expect to be restored. By the grace of a loving Father I have freedom from my past and the guilt and condemnation I inflicted on myself across so many years. I still have pain and other issues, but I know the Lord will take care of me and I have to keep moving forward on his path for my life.

I have been in chiropractic treatment with the doctor I will call Dr. Brad, a holistic chiropractor. He has been documenting my progress with X-rays every few months to track my progression. Which, when I saw the most recent set before an accident in 2014 . . . well, I was amazed and started to cry at the gift of healing from God.

Occasionally the vertebrae in my back will slip out of place, and this makes it hard to walk when my sciatic nerve is pinched. Dr. Brad is a man of God, and through his hands the Lord has been healing many from all of their illnesses through aligning the spine to function as the good Lord intended. He teaches proper nutrition and exercise and, if possible, to eliminate medications, all so we can live healthy lives. I am just one of many people he has helped.

But in June 2014 I was involved in a car accident. As I was driving down West Ashley Avenue on Folly Beach, a woman was preoccupied, looking to see if any spots were available to park while also waiting to make a left turn into the beach access parking area. I was going slowly, as there are many people and animals walking along this street to the beach. I was going east; she was going west. I saw her looking to the left, ready to turn. She had a patrol car in front of her and behind her. As I was about to pass her car she swung in front of me, which stopped me in my tracks. I was in shock as the back of my van went up in the air, I am hurt. To boot, as we sat in our vehicles next to each other, she made no apology. I would have been so apologetic if the roles had been reversed.

I had worked so hard to fight back from so many issues, and I finally had them under control. I had just started walking on the beach near my home. *I had even started to work out in the hopes of getting my muscles strong again. But the accident injured areas I never had issues with in the past.* The atlas in my neck was damaged, and it no longer keeps my back stable as it can pop out and has to be manually pushed back in to relieve the head-aches, stiff neck, and radiating pain that shoots down my back and legs. To say that my limited abilities resulting from this pain has been depressing is an understatement.

With a broken bone in my left foot, injured insteps, and Achilles tendons on both feet, I had to wear a compression boot on my left foot from late July to October 2014. This pain in my feet has been horrible and quite dis-abling; on some days just getting out of bed and walking takes lots of effort. *So the mistake of a stranger has knocked me back to square one. But I believe this too shall pass.* I have learned to take everything with a grain of salt, and to not let my circumstances and pain deter the joy the Lord has given me, as I cannot control the thoughts and actions of others. Life on this earth is a roller coaster of issues. I rely on God to bring me through it all, as He has always done in the past.

I know these things will pass. You see, I have come to know that just be-cause we love and follow Jesus does not mean our lives will be free from trouble, hardship, and financial struggle. It means if we keep God first, and know his promises, *He will bring us through.* Does it mean we will never see a loved one die or become sick? No, it means that his will for our lives will be done while we exist on earth. If He wants us to stay on this earth as his representative, we will make it through anything. *We have to take care of our bodies to as they are not ours but Gods, as the Holy Spirit resides in us always.*

We are lights to shine in the darkest hours to encourage and tell others there is One who saves, heals, and provides for all their needs through his Word.

Am I financially stable? Not yet, but somehow God has provided for every one of my needs. Although I have pain most days than not, I cast it out in the name of Jesus, and I believe in my total restoration. *Having God on my side, I know I will be provided for and, through my darkest hour, I know I will survive.* The day He calls me home I know I will be with the Father and Son in Heaven. My hope is to be given the opportunities to help in these times to win souls home for the Lord. No one needs to perish with Satan; it is all a choice. *I desire for God to use me to reach those who are lost out there just like I was.*

Over the last year I have been compressing my life's belongings and "stuff" down to ten to fifteen plastic containers. I have gone from someone who could not have enough stuff, who loved money, homes, cars, clothes, and jewelry to not caring if I have any of it! To say it has been freeing and exhilarating and sometimes scary is to put it mildly. I have been moving what I thought were my life's treasures from the three homes I lived in. In my possession are the remains of knickknacks from my parents' lives, toys and memorabilia from my son's life, and the remaining treasures I still hold dear. And I am wanting to slim down even more. *Why am I now giving it all away? I feel in my spirit that I am going to move on, and I need a light load.* Do I know where I am going? No! Will I need things for the journey? Yes! After all I have seen with the Lord's provision, I will have all I need when I need it. Thank you, Jesus!

Some people may think all of this is crazy, especially by today's standards of "more is better." But God has called me to give up trusting in worldly possessions and to trust more in how He will provide for me daily. He has a special task for me, just as He has one for you. And He wants it with you being happy, whole, healed, and ready to go—ready to do what God wants me and you to do.

Here is how the Lord works. The week before Christmas 2014, a friend calls and says, "The Lord told me to give you $500." I was blown away because I was out of cash and food for the dog and me. This gave me the opportunity to get the things I needed and send a box of Christmas gifts to my son. And any Mother knows that it tugs at your heart when there is nothing to give at that time of year, but we were used to it.

Then one day after Christmas, I woke up and found a text message on my phone from a friend of fifteen years. He was selling his 40-foot recreational vehicle and looking for the right buyer.

The Lord told him to give it to me for free.

So here is the text I read: *If you had an RV today, would you have a place to park it?* I sat up in bed as I read this text. This was after I was awake and I had said good morning to the Holy Spirit. (I usually say some prayers to start my day.) I texted back: *Yes.* Mind you, I did not have a clue where to put this RV, or how I would even move something that big, but trusting in God as I do, I said yes anyway. My friend texted back: *Then my wife and I would like to give you our RV for free. I was praying about it last night. The Lord told me to give it to you for free.*

The night before receiving that text, I had been watching a prepper show. I had said to God that if all hell is going to break loose as your coming to this world gets closer, I need a bug-out home like an RV! My plan is to travel the road during a difficult, dark time in our country and tell people what God has done for me. I want as many people as possible to know all Jesus has done for my son and me. To show others that by believing in God's promises He has provided for and healed both my son and me.

I had been praying for an RV for years, ever since God laid on my heart that I would be out there for him. Can you imagine getting your prayers answered like that? Welcome to my life. Now, don't think it is a luxury unit. It is a 1988 model that needs work, but it is fully loaded with everything and anything I could want or ask for. It has a washer and dryer, a full shower, and everything else I did not know could be in one of these things!

The pictures were amazing, and I was so overwhelmed that I was ready to leave the minute I set foot in it. We went to see it; my vision had been that of a perfect RV with minor work needed! When I saw the work that it needed to bring it back to life and be road-worthy, I knew I wasn't hitting the road so fast. Being human, I was starting to fret about how hard this would be and asking how was I going to get all this done. This motor home was top of the line in its day. It had all I could need, and I had asked the Lord to provide an RV to live in comfortably as I headed down the road. It sounds like an air ride tractor-trailer purring down the road!

The only problem is I cannot drive it as it is 40 feet long and has more switches than an aircraft! It is now a family bug-out vehicle in case we need to leave the coast in a hurry. I want to head out on the road when the Lord says the magic words I have heard when I needed to change my future to keep my family safe. What are those words? "Get Out Now!" I will know it is time to move . . . where? Jesus will tell me when I need to know. For now, I trust and have the faith of a child and follow his voice wherever it may lead. I know God has a plan for me.

This brings me back to a movie I love, *Faith Like Potatoes*. A farmer in Africa plants potatoes against all odds, believing God's promises that it would rain on his crop to yield potatoes in a famine and drought, so that he can provide for his family and the village of people who believed in his path with God. He had such great faith in the Lord's provisions, that against all odds, and those who told him it wouldn't work, that he would plant a crop of potatoes. The planting would need a considerable amount of water to grow and produce enough food to save his family and feed all the people who lived in his village. Was his faith rewarded with rain? Yes it was, and so he saved his family and all those in his village. This farmer proved that "all things are possible when God is on our side."

I was always the person with a plan, never quit a job unless I had another, and never moved unless I had a place to go. But since this journey with the Lord began I have not had one plan. I don't have a job; I'm on disability, without help to get any of this done. Will the people in my life be guided by God to help me? Maybe. I can honestly say I don't have a clue how what I hope to accomplish will be accomplished. I am pressing to the mark, Jesus Christ, and the dream He has laid on my heart to tell all who do not know Him how He can change lives.

Do I know the Bible backwards and forwards? Not yet, but I'm studying his words. Do I have my life in control? Definitely not! My temper still flares when I don't get my way, or if I see injustice done to innocent animals, children, and people. *Some may ask, "Who do you think you are, to do or say all of this and believe it?" I myself am no one, but with God I am his child.* Jesus spoke to me when I was in great pain crying out to Him to let me die. Instead, He showed me great compassion and grace; He gave me the choice to become part of his family. Jesus knew who I was from the beginning, when He formed me in my mother's womb. His plan for my life has been set in his kingdom. I just had to open the door of my heart when He knocked, and I invited him into my life and my son's life—forever.

Am I 100 percent who He wants me to be? Heck no. However, I love Him with all of my heart, all of my mind, all of my spirit, and his plan consumes my day and life as I work to keep moving forward. The rest is in Jesus' hands, as He is the potter. I am just the clay in his hands.

Am I the perfect Christian? No, I can say with all honesty. But I do have a relationship with Jesus Christ that I have not had with any other human being on the face of this earth. *We talk all day and all night, and I thank Him for never getting sick of me talking his ear off 24 hours a day!* Does He make me apologize when I am wrong or hurt someone's feelings? Yes, He does. Will He guide me through this crazy life? Absolutely. If I am about to do something wrong, I hear Him tell me not to do it. *When I am about to shoot off my mouth stupidly, I hear Him say, "Stay quiet."* When I type an angry letter to someone I think deserves it, He tells me not to send it or to just delete it.

I hear Him. The difference with me now is I listen and I obey! Sometimes He has to tell me a few times, as I am a thickheaded woman, but He does keep saying it, and even yells at me when I resist. Then I understand He is serious, and I obey his word. When I don't listen to Him, I can see the results of my disobedience. I notice how it affects the person I should have said something to, or the opportunity I missed as a result of not listening to his prompts.

As I sit here today, working on this last chapter in this book, I have very limited funds to my name in three separate bank accounts. Each month I am responsible for keeping what's left of my small business and employees going, and I pay all of my monthly bills after that, and then there is not much left. The old me would be in panic mode; the new me is very peaceful. Do I wonder how all of my burdens will be taken care of? Of course I do. But I know Jesus tells us to give Him all of our burdens, and He will give us rest, peace, and security, and I believe He will provide my every need. He has never let me down. I had to come to the lowest point in my life and relinquish all of my will to accomplish what God wants me to do. A loving God promised to heal me, love me, and provide for me and has done so before my eyes for the whole world to see.

In Revelation 12:11 (KJV), the Bible says: "And they overcame him by the blood of the Lamb, and by the word of their testimony; and they loved not their lives unto the death." When I hear this, in my spirit, I take it in this way: this world has come to a very evil time period.

My role in His plan for me is to be, as David would call me, a warrior for the Lord. I have to reach out with the anointing and power fully believing in what the Bible says we all have from the Lord when we are in his will. To help others hear the Good News about Jesus, to be part of his plan to bring his lost lambs back to Him. For this to happen more people have to start telling their testimonies so others can see what God has done for so many people.

He is not dead; He is the living Christ! He will do the same for those who love Him and accept Him into their hearts. Which means when we let go of our fear, doubt, pride, ego, vanity, selfishness, worldly desires, envy, greed, and more, He will give us all He has, like love, peace, joy, serenity, acceptance, and provision. All of these are waiting for those who love Him. Just like what He has done for my son and I: miracle after miracle.

God has said He wants every soul on the face of this planet to make the choice to know his Son, Jesus, so all can be saved no matter what they have done in their past. God desires that no one is left behind. Because the alternative is a very sad one: to live in the darkness and torment that lasts a lifetime once the choice is made.

~

A true heroine in this story is the lady who owns the condo I call my home today. She lives in New York State. Her name in this story will be SR. When SR had just purchased the condo, I was her first tenant, and I have stayed here for 12 of the hardest but most enlightening years of my life. I was allowed to remodel the condo and we moved in; you talk about grace and provision! Wow. I not only had a bedroom and my own bath for the first time in almost a decade, but it was on the marsh, which looks like the ocean at high tide. I also have a nice deck overlooking the marsh and all the comings and goings and antics of the wildlife keep me happy. I love all of the creatures that share my home here; I hear the birds, large and small, in the palm trees. River otters, raccoons, and my favorite, the ducks, live and have their young in the lakes around this complex.

When we moved in rent was on the first of the month and paid on time. Once the illnesses hit and Moose bought his own home and left, I was not able to pay the rent as we had done before. SR knew the truth of how sick I was and yet let me live here in this beautiful place with never a bad word mentioned. This is an example of God's grace and favor. Every year we paint the condo, wash the rugs, and I have done most of the repairs here at no cost to SR.

I love this place because of all the memories, laughs, and the life I shared here with my son. We overcame our past lives and began to live new lives. I overcame what seemed the path to the grave in my very bedroom, I found God here, and this place has been my safe haven while I have continued on my journey.

One day when God blesses me with abundance, I would love to pay SR back for those lost years, but in the meantime my prayer is for her to be abundantly blessed and held in the highest favor God can bestow on her. Once again, this is all God's provision. He does what I cannot do and I believe He will take care of me. Not because I deserve it, but because He loves me and I am his child.

~

My wish for this book is that it is read by more people than I could imagine. Whether to be critical and debunk it, or even just to have a good laugh about it—I don't care. Or maybe to find some peace, hope, and joy in knowing and believing that He will take care of all your needs. That He will heal all of our illnesses and take away our pain and depression that others, or we, have inflicted upon ourselves. That we can ask Him to forgive our sins and He will open the door to us. That we believe and then remember that He died for us so we could be saved from hell. Ask Him to come into your heart and be the Lord and Savior of your life. If we sincerely are repentant He can change us to be godly people from the inside out and so be proud of us. Jesus will come into our hearts and fulfill all the promises He told us about in the Bible. Do we have to be perfect people during this time? Not at all. He will change our thoughts and hearts one day at a time.

He knows we mess up and that we will continue to make mistakes along the way until we go home to Heaven. Being a follower of Jesus Christ is a lifelong journey that doesn't end until we go home to be with Him. He gives us the Holy Spirit to guide us and show us right from wrong. What paths to take or walk away from. The choice is all ours. Once we realize it is not what we can do for Jesus, it is about what Jesus has already done for us, then we will be fine.

Grace and God's love for his children save us. We cannot do anything for God to win his love, like some might think. Good works mean nothing without being saved by God and holding the love of Jesus in our hearts. God loves us unconditionally, and nothing can break us out of his love for us unless we turn our backs on Him. Above all, I have learned to trust in what I cannot see but can hear and feel. I find great peace and security in this thought. All my life I always believed that as long as I could work I didn't need anyone. Well a time came in which I could not work and I had no one, but I did have Jesus. He knows my heart as well as my fears and weaknesses.

In my weakness I rely on Jesus' strength and confidence to stand, and I know He is Lord over all good and evil. *No matter how dark it looks, no matter what your circumstances are, they will not stay that way forever.* Find hope and believe the light of the Lord will reach you no matter where you are or what you are doing. Just reach up for his hand and He will never let you go.

~

Thank you to God for never giving up on me, and please let me hear your voice in my heart guiding me through this world until I come home to you.

To anyone I may have hurt in my past, I am sorry.

To all of those who have forgiven me, thank you!

To Roseanne, who has been my BFF for more than 40 years, I love you!

To Moose and Annie, thanks for being in our lives. Your friendship is very precious to me.

To Cecilia, my sister in Christ, thank you for being the Lord's teacher of the Bible when I did not know the Word of God as I began my relationship with Jesus.

To David and Barbara's family, my family from the Lord: thank you for all the love and guidance throughout the years!

Last but never least, to my son: I am truly blessed and grateful for having your love in my life. You made me a better person by being your mom. You were everything I hoped for when I asked God to give me a child to love; He gave me you. My wish for you is to keep God guiding your life, and also your family. That God will bring you into all He has for your destiny. I ask that your footsteps are kept hidden from evil and protected by the blood of the lamb, Jesus Christ. Most of all I ask God to bring you a love that will last a lifetime and to have the family you have always wanted. You are an amazing man. You will be a loving husband and an awesome father. I pray to the Lord to let me be a part of your future.

I pray, Heavenly Father, that all who read this book gain all the courage and strength needed to overcome every painful season in their lives. To accept your Son, Jesus, into their hearts so their eyes will be open to see your truth.

We must stand up to Satan and say, "NO MORE!" No longer will we listen to his lies! And we will overcome our illnesses, as God wants us all healthy.

Jesus said He gave his people the power the Father gave Him, to go and heal others in his mighty name. The Bible says God wants us to have abundance to the point where our needs are met abundantly so we can pour out blessings abundantly as we are our brothers' keepers! If we stand for God He will stand for us as we trust in the promises of his Son, Jesus Christ. As his followers we are not here to judge anyone but to show them the love of the Lord, to plant the seed of acceptance, tell them the Good News, and leave the rest to the Lord. It is **His** job to judge the sins of others; it is certainly not ours!

Printed in the USA
CPSIA information can be obtained
at www.ICGtesting.com
JSHW012034140824

68134JS00033B/3048